The Devotional
Resource Guide

The Devotional Resource Guide

Joseph D. Allison

THOMAS NELSON PUBLISHERS
Nashville • Camden • New York

Published in Nashville, Tennessee by Thomas Nelson, Inc. and distributed in Canada by Lawson Falle, Inc., Cambridge, Ontario.

Printed in the United States of America

Library of Congress Cataloging in Publication Data

Allison, Joseph D.
  The devotional resource guide.

  Bibliography: p.
  Includes indexes.
  1. Devotional literature—History and criticism.
2. Devotional literature—Abstracts. I. Title.
BV4818.A39   1986   016.242   85-29868
ISBN 0-8407-5950-9 (pbk.)

For James Earl Massey
Dean of the Chapel, Tuskegee Institute
whose life bears the fruit one would expect
of a tree planted beside still water
(Psalm 1:3)

Contents

Preface

Fighting back the tears, she said, "No matter how hard I try, I can't seem to keep my devotional time with the Lord. How can I discipline myself to do that?"

Another member of my congregation asked the common question, "What books would be good to use for my daily devotions?"

An engaged couple said during our premarital counseling sessions, "We want to start having daily devotions together. It's a habit we want to start even before we're married. But *how* do we start?"

These questions express the heartfelt need of many Christians to develop a more meaningful devotional life. Some writers refer to this area of interest as "spirituality"; they call the process of spiritual growth through devotional worship and other means "spiritual formation." Pastors, retreat leaders, and Christian educators are attempting to understand the dynamics of this process, no matter what we call it, because modern Christians feel a burden to have a more intimate relationship with God.

Jacob Needleham, professor of the philosophy of religion at Yale (and a Jew by birth and upbringing), says that Christians of all traditions are seeking a "lost Christianity."[1] His interviews with seminary professors, priests, and laymen of every rank have revealed a pervading hunger to regain the spiritual vitality that seems to have been lost in recent years. Needleham believes we will find it by returning to mysticism. Though I would dispute that conclusion, I agree that everyone interested in the current state of Christianity realizes the need for something better in the typical Christian's spiritual life.

That is why I have written this book: To identify the hunger for a better devotional life and to indicate some ways we might respond to that hunger. I don't think a Christian who genuinely seeks to please the Lord can say that the hunger for spiritual growth is ever satisfied; it's a lifelong appetite that is sometimes keen, sometimes abated, but never fully satisfied. The psalmist says, "O taste and see that the Lord is good" (Psa. 34:8). The devotional life is surely that—*tasting* of the Lord—and the more we taste of the sweet fellowship with him, the more we savor it and the more our spiritual appetite grows.

---

[1]Jacob Needleham, *Lost Christianity* (New York: Bantam Books, 1982).

This book offers some practical suggestions for enriching your devotional life. We will compare several hundred resources you might use for your daily devotional time.[2] I believe this information will help you start having a daily devotional time or, if you already have one, to make that time more meaningful. With this information in hand, you will be better equipped to grow spiritually.

Of course, information and guidance are not enough. A growing devotional life begins with an irrepressible desire to worship God and enjoy his fellowship each day. That desire is more than a burden, the sense that you "ought" to have a devotional time each day. It's a passion (dare I say an *obsession*) to be with God and to grow up "into the measure of the stature of the fullness of Christ" (Eph. 4:13), reflecting God's glory as faithfully as Christ did.

I write this book with the prayer that as it supplies the information you need, God's Holy Spirit will supply a desire to obtain the joy of a growing devotional life.

Joseph D. Allison
Grand Rapids, Michigan

---

[2]I have likewise presented the best Bible study resources in my previous book, *Bible Study Resource Guide*, rev. ed. (Nelson, 1984).

Chapter One
How Are Your Devotions?

With so many Christians talking about "having personal devotions" and "strengthening my devotional life," we would do well to begin this study by asking a basic question: *What is the role of a personal devotional time in a Christian's daily life?*

Well-known Christians affirm the value of a daily devotional time. Martin Luther spent an hour in prayer each morning. John Wesley had a special prayer desk with a kneeling pad and a stand where his Bible could be laid; he spent two hours there each morning, reading and praying. When the late Dr. Frank Gaebelein was asked what advice he would give to the next generation of Christians, he said, "Maintain at all costs a daily time of Scripture reading and prayer."[1] This noted Christian educator and Bible scholar called his daily devotional time "the most formative influence in my life and thought." Missionary and popular writer E. Stanley Jones said that every Christian should cultivate an attitude of receptivity to God. He concluded: "In order to have a continuous state of relaxed receptivity we must have periods of quiet when we gain the poise and power that will go throughout the day. Those who say that they can live in a state of prayer without stated times for prayer will probably find themselves without both. . . . "[2] Gerald Strober describes the beginning of a typical day for evangelist Billy Graham:

> At the Holiday Inn North on Frontage Road, a middle-aged man on his first visit to Jackson [Mississippi] in twenty-three years munches on a piece of toast and watches the "Today" show news report from his top floor suite. There are many things this visitor could do on this lovely morning; . . . but he will not have time to attempt any of these pleasant diversions. In a few minutes he will sit at the bedroom desk and read a well-thumbed copy of the Living Bible; and then, the day's portion of scripture perused and absorbed, he will bow his head and he will meditate upon the many concerns that are on his heart and the multitude of questions that have been put to him for advice and decision; and he will especially remember why he has left the beautiful mountain country of western North Carolina to come

---

[1]Quoted by Gretchen Gaebelein Hull, "Frank Gaebelein: Character before Career," *Christianity Today.* September 21, 1984, p. 14.
[2]E. Stanley Jones, *Abundant Living* (Nashville: Abingdon-Cokesbury, 1942), p. 239.

to this city; and he will think of all the tasks and responsibilities that await him this day; and he will be humbled and finally, as he does each day of his life, he will ask God for strength, wisdom and blessing upon his ministry.[3]

Such testimonies challenge all Christians to devote some time to prayer and quiet communion with the Lord each day. As James Russell Lowell said, "The nurse of full-grown souls is solitude." Every earnest Christian yearns to have some time alone with God, a time of devotional worship.

Yet most modern Christians are frustrated in their efforts to set aside a daily devotional time. Our high-pressure schedules claim our attention before morning coffee has been poured. The incessant demands of family, friends, and the community bid for our thought and energies each moment of the day. We have scant time available for devotions, and the time we do have is pressed between the pages of life's heavy schedule book. This is why the Roman Catholic renewal writer William Callahan has encouraged Christian professional people to cultivate the art of "noisy contemplation," impromptu prayers amid the noisy activities of the day. It is why Ruth Bell Graham and other busy mothers have learned the technique of "praying on the hoof."[4] Such improvised methods seem to be the only ways many Christians are able to turn their thoughts toward God.

Yet when we reflect on the purpose of worship, we realize that these hurried, catch-as-catch-can devotions are sadly inadequate. Devotional time is after all a time of worship, and any type of worship has two primary goals: (1) to glorify God—to reflect God's glory to him and to the world—and (2) to grow up into the fullness of Christ. How effectively does impromptu worship reflect God's glory, to him and to the world? How helpful are extemporaneous devotions in the lifelong process of growing into the likeness of Christ? Devotions-on-the-run have limited value in both respects. By no means do such furtive prayers follow the pattern of Christ himself, who sacrificed his comfort and convenience to spend hours alone with his heavenly Father despite the strident demands of his daily ministry. If we wish to have the depth of spirituality that Jesus had during his public ministry, we must go beyond the "lightning prayers" that flicker through our minds as we swing from the subway strap or the church tunes we hum while we wash the dishes. An honest reading of Jesus' life forces us to admit that devotional worship is far more than this.

Several Gospels tell us that Jesus "rose yet a great while before day" to pray (Mark 1:35; Luke 4:42). He sought seclusion for times of personal worship (Mark 6:46). The Book of Acts demonstrates that the early Christians fol-

---

[3]Gerald S. Strober, *Graham: A Day in Billy's Life* (Garden City NY: Doubleday, 1976), p. 18.
[4]Ruth Bell Graham, "Mercy Suits Our Case," *Decision,* April 1964, p. 9.

lowed this pattern; there we find Cornelius the centurion praying alone in his house (Acts 10:1 ff.) and Peter praying alone on a housetop at midday (Acts 10:9 ff.). In each case, no special feast day or Sabbath seemed to occasion their prayer time; rather they took time out from the duties of an ordinary day to commune with God, as Jesus had done.

I believe modern Christians are turning back to the New Testament to rediscover this pattern for their devotional life. We are beginning to realize that the first century was no less demanding than our own, yet the Christians of that era enjoyed a vital devotional life. Their devotional pattern, rather than being novel, can be normative for the Christian. That seems confirmed by modern Christians such as Gaebelein, Jones, and Graham, whose daily devotions lay the foundation for lives of faithful Christian service and spiritual growth.

We should note that our English word *devotion* comes from the Latin *devovere,* meaning "to pledge or promise." So this daily time of personal worship is not something required of the Christian; rather it is a commitment freely chosen, a promise unilaterally made at the Christian's own initiative. Meaningful devotions begin when a Christian decides to commit his time, energy, and attention to a daily tryst with God.

God promises to meet every Christian who desires to meet with him. "But without faith it is impossible to please Him," the Bible says, "for he who comes to God must believe that He is, and that He is a rewarder of those who diligently seek Him" (Heb. 11:6, NKJV). The word here translated as "diligently seek" (Gk. *ekzeteo*) literally means "to seek with full desire." Thus God's Word promises that he is ready to have fellowship with anyone who genuinely believes he is there and earnestly wants to know him. So our initiative to meet God encounters his immediate response; he is just as eager to meet with us as we with him. The Christian who vows to have a devotional time each day will find the Lord vowing to honor that time with his presence. It is an agreement—a pledge of mutual commitment—a dual devotion of the Christian and his God.

We should note that the devotional vow is *secret.* Jesus praised the private worship of a woman or man of God, in contrast to those who make public vows of fidelity to God in order to gain public recognition (cf. Luke 18:9-14). Have you noticed that Paul never refers to his own devotional life, despite all his exhortations to personal piety? Neither does John (though we catch a glimpse of John's devotional habits when he opens the record of his apocalyptic vision with the words, "I was in the Spirit on the Lord's Day"—Rev. 1:10, NKJV). Jesus and the apostles made their vow of personal worship a *secret* thing. No one else knew the substance of their devotional pledge to God, though everyone could see the results of it.

Second, we find that meaningful devotions begin with a *specific* vow. A Christian who sets a definite time, place, and purpose for his private worship of God is engaging in true "devotions." He fixes clearly in his mind where and why he will meet with God each day as when Gideon put forward a plan for seeking God's will each morning before he entered a decisive battle (Judg. 6:37-40).

Third, we learn from Scripture that genuine personal worship results from a *solemn* vow. The earnest Christian does not plan his devotional time as a casual experiment nor an impulsive imitation of his friends. He makes his devotional time a sincere commitment to God that overrides all other commitments he has. Keeping this commitment will be costly. But as David said, "God forbid that I should give my Lord a gift that has cost me nothing" (2 Sam. 24:24).

Let us consider some practical ways to establish a daily devotional time.

The Right Time and Place

Select a devotional time that is conducive to worship. We might characterize this time in three ways:

First, it should be a time free from *interruptions*. This may be the most difficult part of beginning daily devotions, since most of us live in a world fraught with interruptions. But the fewer the distractions, the more undisturbed can be our communion with the Lord. One young mother accomplishes this by having her devotional time in early afternoon while her youngest children are napping and the rest have not yet returned from school. She disconnects the telephone, switches off the radio and TV, and enjoys a quiet hour of worship. (A fringe benefit of her early afternoon devotions—she's in a much better mood to greet her school-aged children when they burst through the door at 3:30.) A physician in Tennessee goes to his office an hour early each morning and sequesters himself behind the closed door; his answering machine takes the calls. A worker on the auto assembly line in Indiana takes his sack lunch to his car and spends the lunch hour in prayer. Each of these Christians has found an isle of tranquillity, free of interruptions, in the midst of a busy work day.

What hour of your day is least likely to be interrupted? That's a good time to consider for your devotions.

Second, it should be a time that's free from *irritations*. The hour before you go to bed at night may be free from scheduled interruptions; but if your neighbor loudly plays his stereo, you may be frustrated in your efforts to worship. The "siesta hour" after lunch may seem good for your devotional time; but if you have spent lunchtime with an irritating person or in unpleasant surroundings, you may be in a foul mood to worship afterward.

No time can be completely free of irritants, of course. But you can save yourself much frustration if you avoid trying to have your devotions during the most frazzled, nerve-jangling moments of your day.

Third, the devotional time should be free from other *interests*. The early morning is often a good devotional time for this reason. You can converse with the Lord more freely before you start thinking about the errands and appointments that will occupy your day. Even if you choose the early morning for your devotions, you will need to discipline your thoughts toward the Lord. I take a walk around our apartment complex each morning, praying and meditating in solitude. Yet I am often sidetracked by thoughts of the projects waiting on my desk, bills I need to pay, and so on. (I'll have more to say later about how to deal with wandering thoughts.)

Just as important as choosing a time conducive to worship is choosing a place that is well-suited to your daily devotions. We have already seen that it's best to anticipate interruptions, irritations, and distracting interests and find ways to avoid these. The place you choose should help to accomplish these ends. In addition, seek a place that helps you focus on Christ, on eternity, and on release of your human preoccupations. This three-point focus will create an atmosphere that is truly worshipful.

Focused on Christ. The place for your devotions may have a symbol such as a crucifix, a basin and towel, or some other symbol that aids you in focusing on the person of Christ. A portrait such as Warner Sallman's "Head of Christ" or Frances Hook's contemporary sketches of Jesus may establish such a point of focus. A Bible opened to a passage from the Gospels that narrates some event from Jesus' earthly ministry; a poster with a thought-provoking statement about Christ; your prayer diary with its records of the ways God has answered your prayers—these and many other objects may help you center your thinking upon the Lord Jesus Christ.

Retreat directors encourage their retreatants to spend some time in quiet solitude "centering down." There is great benefit in this process of laying aside all other concerns to focus on the essence of your own personality and the image of God within you. The worship symbols that remind you of Christ can assist in centering: centering on the character of the One who is meeting with you.

Focused on eternity. We need to regain a sense of God's perspective on the events of our daily lives. Pushed along by the jostling clangor of each day's events, we forget that God sees the day in the full expanse of his timeless purpose and plan. Natural surroundings help us regain a sense of eternity. Perhaps your neighborhood is favored with a stately oak tree, a bubbling stream, a tranquil pond, or some other center of natural beauty; what better place to breathe deep of the refreshing draughts of God?

I have found that archaic surroundings also help to keep my focus on God's great canvas of eternity. Some of my most delightful hours of devotion were spent in the Carnegie library of my former hometown, a fine example of late

Victorian architecture, its lobby crowned with a dome that looked like a huge inverted bowl of Wedgewood china embellished with blue-and-white rosettes. When I stepped into that lobby, I forgot about the tensions of the day and entered a sanctuary that seemed to transcend all time. Perhaps other kinds of surroundings help you disconnect from the present day. Why not seek those surroundings for your devotional time? By whatever means, learn to cultivate an attitude of temporal detachment and get in touch with the serene ambiance of eternity.

Focused on release. Jesus suggested on several occasions that worship is best done in private (Matt. 6:6). Why? Surely he was not implying that worship should be hidden in shame, nor did he suggest that worship is an elite activity that we should hide from the prying eyes of a "vulgar" public. Rather I think Jesus encouraged us to seek a private place for worship because we can release all social pretensions there. In the prayer closet we do not need to defend our opinions, justify our actions, or try to polish a reputation for ourselves. (We need not do those things in public, either; but how easily we slip into these maneuvers to gain leverage in a group!) Worship should be a time for releasing the self into the hands of God. Privacy helps us do that.

Certain postures of release help as well. Devout people of various religions know the cathartic value of kneeling, lying prostrate, leaning against a massive object (as when the Jews visit the Wailing Wall), and other postures that physically express their helplessness and dependence upon God. Evangelical Christians hesitate to try these postures of worship because they are so closely identified with Judaism, Catholicism, Islam, and Eastern religions. But I believe we ought to learn how to express our dependence upon God; and if such postures help us orient our thinking to that end, let us employ them.

Pastor Oswald J. Smith of The People's Church in Toronto and A. W. Tozer, pastor of a Christian and Missionary Alliance congregation in that city, agreed to meet for morning devotions. "Where do you have your devotions?" Smith asked.

"At the beach on Lake Ontario," Tozer replied. "You can meet me there any morning at 5 o'clock."

Smith did exactly that a few days later. Parking his car at the beachside lot, he noticed Tozer's car was already there, but saw no trace of Tozer himself. Smith began walking along the fog-shrouded beach. Suddenly he came upon the dark form of a body lying in the cool, wet sand. It was Tozer stretched full-length on the beach, his hands resting on an open Bible, its pages fluttering in the pre-dawn breeze. That was how Tozer prayed in private.

Make sure that in some way your surroundings encourage you to let go of your habitual mannerisms and yield yourself to the gracious presence of the Lord.

Clarify Your Agenda

Having considered the preliminaries of time and place, let us think about the purpose of your daily devotional time. What do you intend to do? What is the result you desire? This determines the attitude with which you approach your devotional time, it will guide your selection of materials you will read (if any), and it will help you gauge whether certain devotional practices are appropriate for you. Obviously, I cannot dictate what the purpose of your devotional time should be. Only you can discern that as you prayerfully seek the Lord's will for your devotional life. But let me briefly describe the agenda of my own devotions, as it may spur your own thinking along these lines:

First, I have concluded that my devotional time is not for study in the traditional sense. My purpose is not to analyze a Bible passage or ruminate on some majestic theological concept. That concentrated, systematic, inquisitive type of activity would soon become an end in itself. While learning is vital to my Christian life, I believe my devotions are primarily to express my individual worship of the Lord; that involves my entire being—my body and soul as well as my mind and will.

Second, I believe my devotional time is not primarily to edify myself but to glorify God. He usually edifies me in that process! But I do not evaluate my devotional time on the basis of how I feel afterward or what new knowledge I have acquired; rather I consider what I have offered to God: How much more of me does the Lord now possess? To what extent have I become more like Christ in my thinking and behavior? How faithfully does my life glorify (i.e., reflect the majesty of) God? These are the crucial questions for me.

If I engage in worship out of a sense of duty or in an effort to obtain the spiritual blessing I admire in some other Christian's life, I choke the very life-breath of worship. I come to the hour of worship to present myself to God as a "living sacrifice," ready for him to direct and use. If I come expecting to better myself or even to obtain a blessing (how piously fitting that phrase sounds!), I am bound to be frustrated. Jesus said that God seeks those who will worship him "in spirit and truth" (John 4:24), those who are wholly concerned with pleasing him rather than fulfilling a traditional duty or wresting some kind of reward from God's hand.

Even if you do not agree with my conclusions about the purpose of daily devotions, you have found that a right attitude toward worship does not just "happen." Nor can it be neatly constructed by careful reasoning or dialoguing with other Christians. It is a gift of God. Right purpose, right motive, right attitude toward worship—these are grace gifts. You can find no better place to begin your daily devotions than by praying that God will awaken your heart and mind to the meaning of worship. Ask him to prepare you for worship. Invite him to set the agenda. Expect him to reveal the devotional methods that are most appropriate for you.

Common Problems

Any Christian who embarks on a plan of daily devotions will encounter some difficulties. You can expect to have your share. Here are some of the problems that we commonly meet in the devotional life:

Wandering thoughts. I confessed earlier that I have this problem quite often during my morning devotional walks. Though I approach my devotions fully intending to focus on the Lord, I begin to pick up random thoughts about my job, my family, and personal obligations of various kinds. And so my devotional time degenerates into a half hour of careless musing. Surely you have experienced the same. Thomas R. Kelly writes:

> Lapses and forgettings are so frequent. Our surroundings grow so exciting. Our occupations are so exacting. But when you catch yourself again, lose no time in self-recriminations, but breathe a silent prayer for forgiveness and begin again, just where you are. Offer *this* broken worship up to Him and say: "This is what I am except Thou aid me." Admit no discouragement, but ever return quietly to Him and wait in His presence.[5]

Kelly's counsel works. If you gather up the tangled thoughts and offer them to God the moment you discover your inattentiveness, he can transform them into an offering of praise. Talk with God about that troublesome relationship with your children, that nagging physical ailment, that irascible supervisor, or whatever concern has moved into your thoughts. Invite the Lord to deal with it. Then return to quiet contemplation of the Lord himself.

Here is another way to deal with wandering thoughts: Jot them on a piece of note paper until you have emptied your mind of every concern. The mind stores a great deal of "unrecorded freight," stuff that you have tucked away for future reflection; and when you apply your mind to the serious business of communing with God, the mental inventory tumbles out. It seems as if the mind has to get rid of that subconscious backlog before it can accept anything new. So be it. Jot down the stray thoughts for later consideration. (At first you will be surprised how much you jot down, because the note taking seems to draw out a torrent of additional concerns. But after several moments you will reach a point of catharsis when the mind is free, clear, and relaxed.)

Introspection rather than adoration. Worship moves in two directions: inward in reflection, self-awareness, and confession; and outward in adoration, affirmation, and acceptance of God. No one can reduce the act of worship to a neat formula that shows how one movement leads to another. Indeed, these

---

[5]Thomas R. Kelly, "The Light Within," quoted by Thomas S. Kepler, ed., *An Anthology of Devotional Literature* (Grand Rapids: Baker, 1977), p. 637.

movements occur simultaneously. Both the inward and outward movements are vital to worshiping God. We should not neglect any of these or feel duty bound to hasten from what we think is a less important phase of worship to one that seems more important. Every phase of worship—those that focus inward and those that focus outward—is important.

When we give most of our devotional time to introspection (the inward movement), we undercut the primary purpose of worship. Instead of honoring God, we honor ourselves. This "honor" of self does not necessarily take the form of self-congratulation, either; self-pity and self-recrimination are common ways of honoring the self. Whatever form it takes, too much introspection causes us to forget the reason we came to worship. We push God to the margin of our lives so we can give full attention to analyzing our own strengths and weaknesses.

How can you avoid undue emphasis on this inward movement of worship? Regular worship with a group of other Christians will help. When you blend your voice with the rest of the congregation to sing praise to God, or when you kneel with other Christians to pray about common concerns, you move from searching your own heart to searching the heart of God.

You can also overcome undue introspection by using a prayer list in your daily devotions: Write the names of people who need God's gracious care in various ways—salvation, recommitment to Christ, changing bad habits, physical and spiritual healing, reconciliation with old enemies, or whatever their needs might be. Pray for these people's needs every day. Let your devotional time place you in a kind of spiritual conning tower where you prayerfully sweep the horizon, alert to problems. The more you do this, the broader your spiritual horizons will become.

Exaltation to alienation. Of course it is possible to give undue focus to the outward movement of adoration as well. You can be so rapt in awe of God that you feel alienated from him. That would run counter to the purpose of worship, too.

We begin to realize the problems entailed by such estrangement from God when we remember that we devote ourselves to times of worship for two primary reasons: (1) in order to give God the honor due his name; and (2) to place ourselves in such intimate contact with God that he will be able to transform us, making us more like himself. So if we imagine God is a sovereign who rules from a distance, a cosmic spectator to the events of our daily lives, we will expect no life-changing intimate contact with him. Do you hold such attitudes toward God? Do you find yourself saying with Peter, "Depart from me, Lord, for I am a sinful man" (Luke 5:8)? Then your worship is handicapped.

Conversational prayer is a simple way to begin breaking down the notion that God is alien or remote from you. Simply speak aloud to God as you would to any other friend. Voice your honest feelings about him—your reverence, praise, gratitude, puzzlement, perhaps even anger.

The seventeenth-century French monk Brother Lawrence expanded the idea of conversational prayer into a life-encompassing attitude that he called "practicing the presence of God." He learned to visualize the Lord with him in the most menial tasks of his daily routine, such as washing dishes and preparing meals. He wrote:

> I have quitted all forms of devotions and set prayers but those to which my state obliges me. And I make it my business only to persevere in His holy presence, wherein I keep myself by a simple attention, and a general fond regard of God, which I may call an *actual presence of God;* or, to speak better, an habitual, silent, and secret conversation of the soul with God....[6]

Brother Lawrence conversed with God silently, but he continued the dialogue throughout his busy day. You can talk with the Lord likewise, silently or aloud, and thus begin to realize that the Lord is involved in every aspect of your daily affairs.

The prophet Isaiah learned this through his life-changing moment of prayer in the Temple at Jerusalem (Isa. 6:1 ff.). Standing in the men's court, Isaiah had a marvelous vision of the Lord sitting on his mercy seat in the holiest place of the Temple. He saw the Lord "high and lifted up, and His train filled the temple" (v. 1). Mysterious winged creatures fluttered around God's throne and sang his praises. The flaming altar blazed brightly, filling the Temple with acrid smoke that obscured everything from Isaiah's sight except the awesome figure of God himself, towering above him in regal splendor. And how did Isaiah respond?

> "Woe is me, for I am undone! Because I am a man of unclean lips, And I dwell in the midst of a people of unclean lips; For my eyes have seen the King, The Lord of hosts" (v. 5).

He exalted God to the point of alienation. Yet without denying his truly exalted character, God showed Isaiah that God desires personal communion with the one who worships him. One of the winged creatures snatched a glowing coal from the sacrificial fire of the altar and touched it to Isaiah's lips, saying,

> "Behold, this has touched your lips; Your iniquity is taken away, And your sin purged" (v. 7).

Seldom does one have such stunning visions to portray God's relationship to

---

[6]Nicholas Herman, "How to Practice God's Presence," quoted by Thomas S. Kepler, *op. cit.,* p. 434.

the worshiper. But when we exalt God and deprecate ourselves until we despair of ever being able to know God or please him, he reminds us that his grace makes our worship possible. By virtue of God's sacrificial love we have the privilege of meeting with him in daily devotions and other choice times of worship.

An Invitation

The Lord invites you to a time of intimate communion with him each day. As one of his followers, you have been given the high privilege of meeting privately with God to express your love for him, to seek his counsel, and to share his concern for the needs of others. Though many Christians do not accept this invitation on a regular basis, it is an important lifeline through which a believer can stay refreshed and alive to God's personal leadership.

During his earthly ministry, Jesus had a similar relationship with the Twelve. He often took them aside from the crowds for personal teaching and encouragement.[7] He planned these retreats just before the disciples were to encounter an especially rigorous test. They gained strength for the test and clarity of mind by spending time alone with him under an olive tree, beside a babbling stream, or couched around the dinner table.

Jesus commended others who chose to spend time alone with him. Remember the argument between sisters Mary and Martha when Jesus visited their home in Bethany? While Martha bustled about the kitchen, basting the lamb and kneading bread dough, Mary lingered in the anteroom—perhaps beside the basin she had used to bathe Jesus' feet—where she listened to him recounting the insights he had gathered on his journey. Martha burst out of the kitchen and started scolding Mary: Why was she wasting time at the Master's feet? Why wasn't she in the kitchen, lending a hand with the meal preparations? Martha tried to enlist Jesus' support for her argument. But he calmly said, "Martha, Martha, you are worried and troubled about many things. But one thing is needed, and Mary has chosen that good part, which will not be taken away from her" (Luke 10:41-42).

Are you "worried and troubled about many things," so that you cannot seem to spend a few moments each day in communion with the Lord? He invites you to pause and put down your towel and basin, your kneading board and basting brush, so you can be with him. Your daily chores are necessary, of course;

---

[7] I think there is significance in the fact that he usually took them aside to "a desert place" (cf. Mark 6:31) for these conferences. Without the distractions of the marketplace or the tugging pleas of relatives (e.g., the mother of James and John), the disciples could commune with him undisturbed. We too know him best in the "desert places"—at times and places set aside from the demands of daily living.

dishes must be washed, beds made, meals prepared, and errands run. But the brief moment you devote to uninterrupted communion with the Lord is "that good part" of your day, "which will not be taken away" from you.

Not unless you allow it to be taken away. Mary had good reason to jump to her feet, mutter a word of apology to the Lord, and rush to the household duties that awaited her. Like Martha, she must have felt the pressure of wanting to prepare a tasty meal for her honored guest. (She had the added incentive of seeing her elder sister standing in the doorway, scowling and tapping her foot!) Yet Mary determined that these moments with the Lord would not be taken away from her. She felt the same obligations Martha felt. But she chose to devote this time to the simple act of being with the Lord. The Lord invites you to do that today and every day.

This book describes some methods and resources you can use to enrich the time you devote to the Lord. The following chapters will list devotional books and magazines to help you get started, resources that are readily available and easy to use. But whatever resources you choose in the beginning, resolve now that the "good part" of your day—the part you devote to private worship of the Lord—will not be taken away from you.

ANNOTATED BIBLIOGRAPHY

The following books teach you basic methods of devotional worship, especially methods of prayer and meditation. Further guidance may be found in many of the books listed at the end of Chapter 2.

Anderson, Andy. *Fasting Changed My Life.* Nashville: Broadman, 1977.
Anderson gives his own testimony of the spiritual transformation that the practice of fasting helped to bring to his life. He examines what Scripture says about this seldom-used discipline and shares the comments of other Christians who have begun fasting as a regular part of their devotional life.

Bounds, E. M. *Power through Prayer.* Grand Rapids: Zondervan, 1965.
This forthright exhortation to confident prayer is based on a literal reading of Jesus' many promises concerning prayer. Bounds invites us to take Jesus at his word, without trying to explain away Scriptures that seem too good to be true. Though sophisticated thinkers will not like Bounds's directness and literalism in interpreting the Bible, many Christians have been challenged by this amazing little book.

Clowney, Edmund P. *CM: Christian Meditation.* Nutley NJ: Craig Press, 1979.
Written in response to the then-popular cult of transcendental meditation (TM), which was based on Hindu meditation techniques, this book affirms

that meditation is a vital activity of the Christian's life—yet it contrasts Christian meditation to that of the Hindu and Buddhist traditions. Clowney contends that orthodox Christian faith is not a mystical religion, which seeks an ecstatic exaltation of the worshiper; instead it seeks to recognize and exalt God. This fascinating book subtly contradicts many of the current Roman Catholic studies of the contemplative life. Clowney writes from a staunchly Reformed perspective, yet not in a pugnacious spirit. A very helpful book on meditation.

Crane, Thomas E. *Patterns of Biblical Spirituality.* Denville NJ: Dimension Books, 1980.

Considers the devotional lives of key biblical figures such as Abraham, Moses, and Paul to identify some guidelines for developing a deeper relationship with God. Written by a respected Roman Catholic.

Demaray, Donald E. *How Are You Praying?* Grand Rapids: Zondervan, 1985.

Originally published by Baker Book House under the title, *Alive to God through Prayer,* this book has been somewhat revised and expanded. Demaray offers a sound introductory chapter on the need for prayer and the basic biblical principles of prayer. The rest of the book is a series of chapters on specialized types of prayer, such as prayer for healing, for family needs, for church problems, and so on. This is a very practical book, simply written.

Dunnam, Maxie. *The Workbook of Living Prayer.* Los Angeles: Acton House, 1974.

This book leads you through a six-week course in prayer with simple daily exercises that include Scripture readings, devotional readings, and instructions in the various phases of common prayer. Ideal for someone beginning a devotional time. Dunnam is pastor of a United Methodist congregation in Memphis and former director of prayer life and fellowship for the Upper Room of Nashville.

Edwards, Tilden H. *Spiritual Friend.* New York: Paulist Press, 1980.

Edwards re-examines the role of the spiritual director, whom Roman Catholics have long trusted to be a friend and counselor in the process of spiritual growth. The author exposes some of the problems and dangers involved with seeking a spiritual director, yet he advocates a renewed emphasis on this worker's contribution to every Christian's spirituality. He helpfully contrasts the spiritual director's task to those of a psychiatric counselor, a pastor or priest. Rich in psychological insight as well as spiritual insight.

Evans, Colleen Townsend. *Give Us This Day Our Daily Bread.* Garden City NY: Doubleday, 1981.

Petitionary prayer—outright requests for physical needs such as food, clothing, healing, and reconciliation—is the focus of this popular little book. Evans deals with the attitudes and conditions that should come before petitionary prayer. She also considers the problem of prayers that seem not to be answered. A practical book that is easy to understand.

Foster, Richard J. *A Celebration of Discipline.* San Francisco: Harper and Row, 1981.

Perhaps the most widely read modern book on devotional practices, this study surveys a great variety of methods for enhancing one's spiritual life. Devotional reading, prayer, meditation, fasting, simplicity of lifestyle—these are just a few of the topics that Foster considers. Recommended as an introduction to devotional practice. This would be an excellent resource for group study as well as individual study, for mature Christians as well as new believers. Foster has written as a sequel, *The Freedom of Simplicity* (San Francisco: Harper, 1981) that explores one of these disciplines in greater detail. Foster is a Quaker.

Freer, Harold W. and Frances B. Hall. *Two or Three Together.* New York: Harper and Row, 1977.

A manual for starting and conducting small prayer groups. Shows how Christians can find mutual support and spiritual growth through such groups.

Grou, Jean Nicholas. *How to Pray,* trans. by Joseph Dalby. Nashville: The Upper Room, 1973.

Here is a new translation of a classic (two-hundred-year-old) book on the practice of prayer. A Jesuit priest, Grou advised his students to learn the art of silent prayer, allowing God to speak. "Grou once remarked that the greatest gift God gave him was a childlike and trusting spirit" (Kepler, p. 526). That simplicity is reflected in this brief and practical guide to silent prayer.

Hamilton, Neill Q. *Maturing in the Christian Life: A Pastor's Guide.* Philadelphia: Westminster, 1984.

What are the marks of a maturing Christian and how can a pastor encourage his or her people to grow spiritually? Hamilton capably deals with these questions in a book packed with practical suggestions for assisting Christians through the various phases of Christian growth. Hamilton teaches New Testament at Drew University. In this book, he does not accept the current psychological theories of faith development, but seeks a more clearly biblical understanding of the process.

Helleberg, Marilyn Morgan. *Beyond TM.* New York: Paulist Press, 1980.

This book stands in clear contradiction to Clowney's at several points; I believe you should read both in order to appreciate the various principles and methods of meditation that Christians hold today. Helleberg favors an introspective type of meditation that seeks the cleansing of ungodly attitudes, habits, and ideas so that the worshiper becomes aware that he is fully absorbed into the being of God, assuming his qualities and virtues. Helleberg provides several meditative exercises designed to heighten one's awareness of God's presence and his redemptive love. A simple, practical, and compassionately written book.

Jennings, Theodore W., Jr. *Life as Worship: Prayer and Praise in Jesus' Name.* Grand Rapids: Eerdmans, 1982.

This book by a professor at Candler School of Theology, Emory University, is a refreshing contemplation of the way in which a Christian's life is devoted to worshiping Jesus Christ—in public prayer, private prayer, solitude, corporate praise, and many devotional activities. Jennings draws upon the theological ideas of Karl Barth, Ernst Kasemann, and other progressive thinkers to create a book that will challenge any thoughtful Christian to re-examine the rationale for his devotional activities.

Keller, W. Phillip. *Taming Tension.* Grand Rapids: Baker, 1979.

From his long experiences on the missionary compound and in other high-pressure ministry situations, Keller describes some methods he has found effective in staving off the crushing demands of life. He underscores the importance of a daily devotional time and a close relationship with the Lord.

Kelsey, Morton T. *Adventure Inward.* Minneapolis: Augsburg, 1980.

This may be the best guide to keeping a spiritual journal. Professor Kelsey explores the history of journal-keeping, some of the practical techniques of journaling, and how the journal writer can incorporate this practice into a well-rounded devotional life.

Kelsey, Morton T. *God, Dreams, and Revelation.* Minneapolis: Augsburg, 1974.

This book investigates what Christians across the centuries have learned about dream interpretation. Some readers will object to the liberal application of modern psychology; others will object to the significance attributed to biblical dream interpretation. Yet the book confronts every serious Christian with an aspect of spirituality that should be better understood.

Laplace, Jean. *An Experience of Life in the Spirit,* trans. by John R. Mooney. Chicago: Franciscan Herald Press, 1977.

A ten-day course of spiritual development based on Ignatius's *Spiritual Exercises,* Laplace's book offers more practical advice on prayer and meditation than Karl Rahner's *Spiritual Exercises.* It is also less theologically sophisticated. Suitable for retreat groups or individual study, this gives traditional Roman Catholic interpretations of the role of the Eucharist and other liturgical exercises in spiritual growth.

Lloyd-Jones, D. Martyn. *Spiritual Depression: Its Causes and Cure.* Grand Rapids: Eerdmans, 1965.

Like Tournier's *The Adventure of Living,* this book provides a helpful explanation of the emotional dynamics of a Christian's life. Lloyd-Jones gives helpful illustrations from his work as a physician. The book focuses on a common problem, depression, and shows how spiritual growth can aid the Christian in dealing with this recurrent difficulty.

Massey, James Earl. *Spiritual Disciplines.* Grand Rapids: Zondervan, 1985.

Here Dr. Massey concentrates on four disciplines of the Christian life— prayer, fasting, dialogue, and worship—exploring in depth the theological and psychological principles of each. Though he does not deal with the great variety of disciplines found in Richard J. Foster's *Celebration of Discipline,* he is able to discuss these four disciplines in greater detail. This book was first published in 1971 by Warner Press under the title, *The Hidden Disciplines.* Written in a serious and thoughtful manner.

Merton, Thomas. *New Seeds of Contemplation.* New York: New Directions Books, 1972.

This book outlines the values of a contemplative life. It encourages all Christians to serve Christ through prayer, meditation, and spiritual reading. Merton was a prominent Roman Catholic writer of the twentieth century. Though some of his later work moved toward universalism (Merton was deeply impressed by the writings of Buddhist contemplatives), his earlier works such as this have lasting appeal for even the most conservative Christian.

Merton, Thomas. *Thoughts in Solitude.* Garden City NY: Doubleday, 1968.

A good introductory study of the devotional value of solitude, Merton's book is primarily for monks and others formally committed to the contemplative life, but it contains rich insights for other Christians as well. It can be easily understood by those who live outside the monastery walls.

Mitchell, Curtis G. *Praying Jesus' Way.* Old Tappan NJ: Fleming H. Revell, 1977.

Mitchell examines the prayer life of Jesus, as recorded in the Gospels, to extract some principles that will enrich the prayer life of every Christian. A book of expository messages, this has very practical value for one's devotional life. Perhaps the best modern study of what the Gospels say on this subject.

Morgan, G. Campbell. *The Practice of Prayer.* Grand Rapids: Baker, 1971.

First published in 1906, this small book has gone through numerous printings and may well be considered a classic manual on the practice of prayer. Morgan explains that our prayers depend on the mediating work of Jesus Christ, now being effected by the Holy Spirit within each believer. So the one who prays must be in submission to Christ and open to the ministry of his Spirit.

Murray, Andrew. *With Christ in the School of Prayer.* Westwood NJ: Fleming H. Revell, 1953.

First published in 1886, this book stands beside G. Campbell Morgan's as one of the great modern guides to practical prayer. Murray divides his work into thirty-one lessons, making it a month-long study. He encourages us to forget our selves and all that we wish to gain through prayer, yielding to the direction of God, allowing him to accomplish what he wishes in our prayers. This book shows the influence of the Deeper Life Movement (in which Murray was active), an interdenominational effort to regain the power of a Spirit-filled life.

Nouwen, Henri J. M. *With Open Hands.* Notre Dame IN: Ave Maria, 1972.

The generous use of dramatic photos in this book gives the first impression that it is another superficial "gift book" of inspiration. But it is more. Nouwen explains that authentic prayer requires openness to both God and our fellow man, and he describes some of the attitudes that we must restrain or set aside to permit this openness to emerge within us. A thought-provoking book by one of the most widely respected of modern Roman Catholic devotional writers.

Rahner, Karl. *Spiritual Exercises,* trans. by Kenneth Baker. New York: Herder and Herder, 1965.

This book grew out of retreats that the author (a German Roman Catholic professor) held for candidates to the priesthood, centering upon the *Spiritual Exercises* of Ignatius. Rahner quotes key passages from Ignatius and applies them to the spiritual challenges that modern Christians must face.

Sanders, J. Oswald. *Enjoying Intimacy with God.* Chicago: Moody, 1980.

While other books in this listing tend to focus on the methods of devotional activity, this book reminds us of its purpose—to find and maintain an intimate relationship with God. Written in a pastoral spirit, this book helps us perceive the depth of our communic   with God. The hinderances that may be obstructing our spiritual growth, and the positive value of a disciplined devotional life.

Santa-Maria, Maria L. *Growth Through Meditation and Journal Writing*. New York: Paulist Press, 1983.

Psychologist C. G. Jung proposed that many psychological disorders of adults are actually symptoms of an inner struggle to find peace with God. Dr. Santa-Maria, a modern Roman Catholic psychotherapist, picks up that thesis and explains how spiritual journal-keeping can help the emotionally or mentally disturbed person carry out his spiritual quest. Written on a more theoretical level than Kelsey's book, this volume offers some novel opinions about the therapeutic value of journal writing.

Sheen, Fulton J. *Lift Up Your Heart*. Garden City NY: Doubleday Image Books, 1955.

Former professor at the Catholic University of America, known to millions of Americans as host of a weekly devotional television series in the 1940s and 1950s, Bishop Sheen was able to express religious truths in terms that a layman could understand. This book describes the spiritual journey from self-centeredness to a life centered on God. Sheen explains quite simply the steps of personal examination, confession, and discipline that one can take to find spiritual peace. It might be called a modern version of Climacus's *Ladder of Divine Ascent,* except that Sheen avoids the mystical speculation and theological complexity.

Stedman, Ray C. *Jesus Teaches on Prayer.* Waco TX: Word, 1975.

A popular conference leader and an innovative pastor, Stedman brings the common man's touch to this study. Not as careful to analyze the Bible evidence as Mitchell's *Praying Jesus' Way,* this book is nonetheless thoughtful and full of practical insights.

Tournier, Paul. *The Adventure of Living,* trans. by Edwin Hudson. New York: Harper and Row, 1965.

Accustomed to writing on a more intellectual plane, psychologist Tournier here turns to the practical problem of finding enjoyment in everyday life, despite its difficulties and spiritual flaws. This encouraging book offers helpful insight into the emotional peaks and valleys of a Christian's life.

Tozer, A. W. *Five Vows for Spiritual Power.* Camp Hill: Christian Publications, 1971.

Though brief, this book explains some basic steps any Christian might take toward a more fruitful life of discipleship. Tozer criticizes the spiritual laxity among most Christians, demonstrating from Scripture that our Lord expects more sacrificial commitment from us—and promises more abundant blessing if we are committed to him.

Ulanov, Ann and Barry. *Primary Speech: A Psychology of Prayer.* Atlanta: John Knox, 1982.

"Prayer, as this book contemplates it, is primary speech. It is that primordial discourse in which we assert, however clumsily or eloquently, our own being. If we are ever honest with ourselves, it is here that we must be..." (pp. vii-viii). Beginning with this premise, the Ulanovs set out to explore the psychological dynamics of prayer. They conclude that self-forgetful prayer is psychologically therapeutic, regardless of the spiritual nurture (or lack of it) that one finds here. This is a most unorthodox yet enlightening study of prayer.

Chapter Two
Devotional Classics

I notice that many Protestant pastors have begun reading the Desert Fathers. Some were required to read these classics as part of a formal course of study. Still others began this reading by chance. Whatever their reasons, I am intrigued to see Protestant ministers who are chary of anything else Roman Catholic now reading and enjoying devotional classics that are deeply rooted in the Roman tradition. Laypersons have a perennial interest in these classics, too.

We have a number of Protestant devotional classics as well. *Pilgrim's Progress,* by John Bunyan; *Hind's Feet on High Places?,* by Hannah Hurnard; *The Christian's Secret of a Happy Life,* by Hannah Whitall Smith; and *My Utmost for His Highest,* by Oswald Chambers are among the devotional works that laypersons cherish generation after generation.

What draws Christians to books such as these? Is it the charm of archaic writing? The allure of an exotic place and time?

Perhaps the style and setting do influence our choice of the classics. But more often, I think, we recognize that God did something extraordinary in the lives of the people who wrote them; we sense that God may use their writings to touch our lives as well. The devotional classics point the way to a deeper relationship with the Lord. Elton Trueblood stressed this in a conversation with Maxie Dunnam several years ago. Dunnam had just been appointed Director of Spiritual Life and Fellowship for the Upper Room (a United Methodist ministry headquartered in Nashville, Tennessee). He sought Dr. Trueblood's counsel soon after his appointment. "If you were given this assignment for ministry," Dunnam asked, "what would you do?" A smile lit Trueblood's face as he replied, "However you do it, Maxie, try to motivate people to *soak their souls in the great models.* Get them to live with the saints, the classic books of prayer and spiritual pilgrimage."[1]

In this chapter we will survey the devotional writings from various periods of Christian history and consider how each of these books can enrich our own spiritual lives.

---

[1]Maxie Dunnam, *The Workbook of Living Prayer* (Los Angeles: Acton House, 1974), p. 122.

What Is a Classic?

What makes a devotional book a "classic"? Certainly we should consider its ability to continue inspiring readers generation after generation, long after its first publication. We should also consider the book's evidence of divine inspiration. Though not in the same sense in which he inspired the biblical writers of old, God does continue to inspire Christian writers; and we can see evidence of that in the classics, which seem to be a natural channel for the Holy Spirit's ministration to us.

But I think there is another vital qualification. I think a devotional classic is marked by its focus on eternal issues that transcend the immediate concerns of the writer. For example, when Brother Lawrence writes about cultivating a sense of God's personal presence in the monastery kitchen as well as in the chapel, he is discussing a need that is just as pressing for Christians today as it was in his century. I believe that makes his writing a devotional classic. When Archbishop Fenélon counsels the ladies of the French court about how to maintain attitudes of humility and simplicity in the midst of their social frills and finery, he is addressing an eternal issue. And so I believe he is writing a classic.

Some will disagree with me at this point. But I believe this feature most vitally affects the impact and longevity of a devotional book: How well does it address the matters that have always concerned us and will concern us until the Lord returns?

This is the chief criterion I have used in selecting certain devotional book classics for the bibliography at the end of this chapter. I believe it is the most telling mark that will separate some modern devotional books from the rest and make them tomorrow's "classics."

I. The Patristic Period (A.D. 30—ca. 400)

In the four centuries following the resurrection of our Lord, the church was led by a succession of great devotional writers commonly called "the church fathers" or simply, "the Fathers." Some of these men held prominent positions of leadership as bishops, primates, or popes; others lived in obscurity as village clerics or monks. But all of the Fathers were prolific writers. Their letters, homilies, and doctrinal treatises were circulated from church to church with growing esteem. Consider the circumstances in which they wrote:

From the beginning of the patristic era, Roman emperors tried to quash the infant church with wave after wave of bloody persecution, beginning with Nero's tortures of Christians in the capital city about A.D. 90. The most prominent church leaders—including several that we classify among the Fathers, such as Clement of Rome and Tertullian—were put to death for their faith in Jesus Christ. Thus much of the patristic era might be called the period of the martyrs. Even the church fathers who had won the admiration of secular leaders were tortured for their convictions; yet they continued to write boldly in defense of their faith. After the conversion of Emperor Constantine (ca. A.D. 312), the Roman Empire granted legal sanction to the church; and Christianity entered a period of peaceful prosperity. Secular powers became cordial to the church and began contributing their treasures to its propagation. Then the church entered the medieval period, in which church and state served one another's interests. As we shall see later, the church then became more highly structured; charismatic church leadership was less likely to emerge; and the official church leaders were less likely to write thoughtful works of devotion.

But let us focus for a moment on the patristic era. Patristic devotional writers tended to be well-educated and wealthy men who could circulate freely in the courts of imperial power. Even in times of martyrdom, the church fathers were respected for their great learning, which was evident in their ability to challenge pagan philosophers with incisive logic. Some served as tutors to the imperial household, even while the emperor waged the most bitter campaigns to exterminate the Christians.

How could the church fathers explain their Christian faith to a pagan, hedonistic culture? They confronted this challenge in at least three arenas:

1. the academic arena, where pagan philosophers defied them to explain Christianity in an objective, persuasive way;

2. the royal arena of inquisitive kings, queens, and patrons who accepted the prevalent secular thinking but were curious about this novel religion called Christianity; and

3. the public arena of merchants, craftsmen, peasants, and slaves who were so intent upon survival that they scarcely gave thought to spiritual or philosophical matters.

The church fathers addressed much of their writing to the first two arenas. If they could change the anti-Christian bias there, the gates of freedom might be opened to allow Christians to worship publicly, establish academies, and continue the evangelistic efforts that had been forced underground at the death of the apostles.

However, the church fathers did not restrict their efforts to scholars and kings. They felt a pressing need to develop a uniquely Christian style of worship apart from the pagan mystery cults, the nominal state religion, and the increasingly ritualized Jewish synagogue worship. So their letters to the churches dealt with the proper significance of liturgical symbols, hymns, and prayers. The Fathers customarily issued encyclicals (i.e., letters to be circulated to all the churches) at Christmas and Easter, in which they called the faithful to observe the Lord's Supper, fasting, and other distinctly Christian worship patterns.

Another concern that compelled the Fathers to write lay letters and treatises was the issue of church polity: Should there be a spiritual and/or administrative hierarchy in the church? If so, what should be the basis of this hierarchy? What should be the prerogatives of each office? As much as creedal issues, this problem of church polity led the Christian church to convene the great councils of Nicea (A.D. 321), Chalcedon (A.D. 451), and Constantinople (A.D. 533), which formalized the episcopal polity of the Eastern and Western churches and marked the end to the patristic era.

With these issues as the backdrop, we can better understand the contents of the patristic devotional classics that have come to us.

First, we notice that patristic devotional writing tends to be exhortative; the Fathers wrote to challenge unbelievers to have faith in Jesus Christ and to encourage beleaguered Christians to hold fast to that faith. These writings have a paternal spirit; they take the form of fatherly advice that a spiritual elder gives to his flock. They are often dialectic, i.e., comparing Christian and pagan ideas side-by-side to demonstrate the merits of Christianity. We find this dialectic approach in many of the patristic letters, as well as in the apologetic treatises where we would expect it.

Modern Christians avoid patristic literature because its style is ponderous and its concerns seem foreign to twentieth-century Christian life. But if we take a closer look at the patristic classics, we find they have real value at several points:

1. Meeting the philosophical challenge. Orthodox Christian faith is being challenged again today by antagonistic philosophies which attempt to reconstruct our understanding of the world on a humanistic basis without God, or which redefine God in an unbiblical, rationalistic way. To meet this challenge, we should reconsider the spirit of patristic writings. The Fathers were able to defend orthodox Christianity in a well-reasoned, dispassionate way that won the admiration of their most bitter antagonists. We would do well to imitate their spirit.

2. Meeting the challenge of social prestige. Unlike the evangelical Christianity of colonial America, which was a religion of the poor, modern evangelicalism, has largely become a religion of the well-heeled and upwardly mobile classes. Evangelicals now mingle with other people of wealth and influence. This gives us a greater opportunity to shape public policy and transform social custom. But for the privilege of rubbing elbows with the rich and famous, we are expected to conform to prevailing upper-class tastes and standards of conduct. The church fathers remind us that such a climate need not chill a Christian's spirituality.

3. Recovering from individualistic religion. Sociologists called the 1970s the "Me Decade" because it was a time when Western society extolled the virtues inherent in oneself. We made a virtual cult of self-discovery and self-fulfillment. The church followed this trend, but Christians found that individualistic religion was really a dead-end street. When they attempted to

construct their own ethical standards and their own basic theology, they set themselves adrift on a stormy tide. Besides the personal disillusionment of this misguided religious "creativity," they were perplexed to see their more "relevant" church was in chaos. The fashionable church of the 1970s roiled with conflicting moral standards, conflicting styles of worship, and combative doctrinal convictions—all of which can be traced to the individualism that we cherished so much. Christians are entering an era of new respect for authority both in their personal relationship with God and in the conduct of church life. We are recognizing the legitimate role of spiritual elders among us. We respect and respond to paternalism (in the best sense of that word) on the part of our elders. At this point, we should re-examine the healthy spirit of paternalism shown in the writings of the church fathers. Theirs was not an overbearing authority but the accepted authority of a recognized gift and calling. Their letters exude a spirit of humility and dependence on God, which did not mitigate their boldness. The emerging spiritual elders of modern evangelicalism would do well to take the Fathers as models. The rest of us could learn from the patristic classics how to identify and follow such elders.

  II. The Medieval Period (ca. 400—1350).

  We are accustomed to calling this long era of church history stretching from the fifth to the fourteenth centuries "the Dark Ages." Yet significant.changes were stirring within the church at this time; indeed, the spiritual legacy of the medieval period influences the life of every Christian today. Some of the most inspiring devotional works were written at this time.

  The Roman Empire became Christian in name—its official title after Charlemagne's coronation was the Holy Roman Empire. Each new emperor swore his allegiance to God and church; thus the rulers came to be called "Confessors." A primate of the church could veto the state's choice of a new king and could ban from Christian fellowship any king who defied church law.

  Yet secular rulers did not always follow Christian standards in ruling their subjects. (Nor can we say the leaders of the church always behaved honorably in dealing with the monarch; but that is another matter.) The medieval period became one of great oppression and civil unrest, despite the supposed partnership of church and state. Landowners extorted bread from the poor. Nobles seized any property (including church property) that helped to consolidate their economic power.

  After the Battle of Tours, the Christian rulers of Europe sealed an uneasy truce with the Muslim rulers of Africa and Spain, opening the door to mutual trade of all kinds—including the trade of philosophical and cultural ideas. Historians agree that Europe's contact with the armies of Islam spelled the end of the medieval period. It began a brief period of "cultural shock" that would give way, three centuries later, to a Renaissance of Western cultural ideals. But I think we have not fully realized the immediate impact that Islam had upon

Christianity. Islamic scholasticism prompted the doctors of the church—respected Christian thinkers such as Thomas Aquinas—to turn from revelation to rationalism as the best way to apprehend the truth about God. This may seem an irrelevant tangent to our discussion here. But as we shall see, Christianity's shift to scholasticism and eventually to rationalism had a profound effect on the spirituality of the church and evoked several new strands of devotional writing. So the Islamic contact should be mentioned here.

Monasteries flourished during the medieval period. The monastic movement had begun late in the patristic era with the establishment of Christian academies in Egypt, Asia Minor, and Italy—houses of study where aspiring young theologians could live with revered spiritual mentors such as Philo, Tertullian, and Gregory of Nyssa. As secular rulers began seizing church properties and taking a more decisive role in selecting the titular heads of the church, the monasteries became the last remaining sanctuaries where Christian leaders could cultivate deeper spirituality and broader Christian service. Religious teaching continued in the monasteries. They also served as the depositories of valuable manuscripts, dormitories for village priests, and chapels for peasants who had no other place to worship. Some of the boldest preaching of the medieval period was done in the monastery chapel. (When monastic preachers such as Savonarola ventured to take their message to the streets during the Renaissance, they were burned as heretics—or they joined the ranks of the Reformers.) Monasteries were the only safe haven for Christians of conscience during the medieval era. For this reason, many medieval devotional classics came from the pens of monks: Roman Catholic, Eastern Orthodox, and (to a lesser extent) the Desert Fathers.

These devotional writers dealt with several new challenges: How could they guide secular rulers (especially the nominally Christian rulers, the Confessors) toward governing their people with Christlike compassion? How could church leaders preach a gospel of freedom to serfs and peasants, yet uphold a secular order that required submission to cruel overlords? How could they proclaim Christian truth in an age of superstition? These new challenges affected the contents of medieval devotional writing.

Devotional classics of the Middle Ages tended to be more reflective than discursive; they focused on the inner discoveries of faith more than on a public defense of it. This reflective mood is quite evident in the monastic rule books written by Bernard of Clairvaux, Francis of Assisi, and others. These books emphasized a very practical approach to spiritual growth with specific instructions for meditation, prayer, and other spiritual exercises that an aspiring Christian might use to draw nearer to God.

In contrast to these devotional writings, yet just as clearly influenced by the challenges of medieval life, were the Christian scholars' attempts to explain the nature of God in logical terms. Dionysius the Areopagite, Anselm of Canterbury, Thomas Aquinas, Roger Bacon, and a host of other Christian scholars tried to fashion a reasonable faith in their treatises on the existence and character of God—a direct response to the rationalistic temper of the age. Their philosophy grew out of their own devotional encounters with God. Instead of constructing a new faith in God, they were trying to articulate their old experience of God in a new way. They were striving to persuade skeptics with their logic; yet they pointed to a personal experience of God as the ultimate confirmation of their logical arguments. So here and there we find that even the medieval scholars contributed to our treasury of devotional classics.

The Middle Ages brought the first substantive writing by the contemplatives, men and women who devoted their lives to ministries of solitary prayer and meditation. Hildegard of Bingen, Meister Eckhart, and other contemplatives recorded their insights in manuals of instruction that enriched the spiritual soil of the church before the flowering of great contemplative movements during the Renaissance.

So what may we gain by reading the devotional classics of the Middle Ages? I believe the Christian scholastics challenge us to articulate our faith in clear, logical terms that will lead us into dialogue with unbelievers. (We normally think devotional life is the very antithesis of rational faith; but the writers of the Middle Ages prove otherwise. An intimate relationship with the Lord compelled them to write monumental works of religious philosophy. That relationship led them to articulate uniquely insightful concepts about the nature of the created order, so that even confirmed atheists must read Aquinas and Bacon with respect.) We should regain the creative dynamic that couples devotional ardor with rational clarity.

A renewed emphasis on the contemplative life would be another benefit of reading the medieval classics. Caught up in our frenetic modern lifestyles, we have lost touch with ourselves and with the presence of God. In this respect, we have more in common with medieval Christians than we may realize; for they were so preoccupied with the crises of war, famine, political intrigues, and epidemics that they began to drift away from their spiritual moorings. The contemplatives called them back. I believe the contemplative writers can perform a similar service for us, drawing us apart from the frantic daily routine to commune with the Lord in devoted solitude.

III. Renaissance and Reformation (ca. 1350—1700)

The Black Plague (1348-51) devastated Europe and scrambled the neatly delineated borders of feudal society. With their labor force decimated by the plague, the sprawling feudal manors could not survive. A new form of city-state emerged as the remaining farmers and day laborers flocked to the towns established by skilled craftsmen and merchants; together they constructed the first burgs, the models of Western urban society.

Europe's contact with the East through the journeys of Marco Polo, the Crusades, and the Muslim invasions brought a revival of interest in Greek and Roman classical culture. This was followed by a new wave of humanistic philosophy, in which the leading thinkers of Europe became deists or agnostics. The Greco-Roman renaissance also brought a new era of realism in art, as Michelangelo and other sculptors recaptured and surpassed the brilliance of the artisans of ancient Rome and Athens. The rediscovery of classical geometry and the brilliant insights of Arabic mathematics kindled a wildfire of progress in science and technology. This was the age of Copernicus, Galileo, Leewenhoek, and Lavoissier.

Religious turmoil rocked the church throughout the Renaissance. Hus, Wycliffe, Luther, Calvin, Knox, and other popular leaders tried to purge the church of mercenary corruption and dogmatic stagnation; when the pope and his episcopal colleagues refused to comply, the Reformers circumvented the usual structures of authority to begin remolding church policy on a popular level by making vernacular translations of the Bible, reinterpreting the significance of the Mass, and publishing repudiations of canon law. Protestantism emerged from the Western church as a result of this turmoil. So the Renaissance brought religious as well as cultural ferment.

Because this was a time of comparative peace in the Mediterranean region and Europe, and because better roads and shipping lanes had been established, the Renaissance was a time of burgeoning commerce. A student of Renaissance architecture sees the impact of this commerce in the great seventeenth-century cathedrals of Mexico City and LaPaz, where Italian wood figures covered by Spanish gold leaf stand on native Latin American granite pedestals. Merchant ships churned the waters of every port, bringing new goods and new profit for their masters.

How could Christian leaders arrest the attention of merchants and craftsmen—the new middle class—who were forsaking what seemed to be an ephemeral religion for the exciting materialistic challenges of their daily trade? How could they influence secular government with Christian values? (A doubly difficult task, considering the intolerance and ruthlessness of many church leaders themselves.) How could Christians communicate God's Word to the common man, amid widespread abandonment of the Greek and Latin versions of Scripture—not to mention the abandonment of Greek and Latin liturgies? Such were the peculiar challenges of the age.

Devotional writers responded with some of their most innovative yet enduring work. In the West, several notable German and Dutch devotional writers emerged at this time; among them were Johannes Tauler, Jan van Ruysbroeck, Heinrich Suss, and Gerhard Groot. In the East, after the fall of Constantinople fragmented the Orthodox church into dozens of small national churches, we find a surge of Byzantine monastic writing and renewed use of encyclical letters by patriarchs who wanted to exhort and strengthen their scattered Christian flocks.

We detect some important changes in the outlook of devotional writers during the Renaissance:

First, they were dubious about Christianity's ability to shape the secular world. The church had exerted a powerful influence over secular affairs in medieval times, so that some Christian thinkers thought they might gradually sanctify the entire world order (e.g., Augustine's *City of God*). Renaissance writers doubted that. They had seen that alliances between church and state tended to secularize the church more than they Christianized the state. Renaissance devotional writers did not conclude that Christian principles were less valid or less resilient; rather they concluded that the secular order was incorrigible. For this reason...

Second, they retreated into an individualistic faith. At the risk of exaggeration, we could say that the Renaissance devotional writers embraced a kind of "closet Christianity," which emphasized private and solitary worship of the Lord. This individualistic faith even moved into the monasteries and convents. In contrast to the original monastic orders, which insisted on a rhythm of worldly involvement and godly detachment, the Renaissance monasteries began emphasizing prayer and study within their sanctuary walls. One might speculate that if the incendiary rhetoric of a Luther or Zwingli had not provoked such an outspoken Catholic response, monastic preaching may have died out during this period. Speculation aside, it is clear that the shift toward individualism and solitary contemplation prompted the pope to approve Ignatius Loyola's Jesuit order and other new religious orders that concentrated on the worldly involvements of preaching, teaching, care for the sick, and so on. These changes reflected a widespread trend toward individualistic religion.

Third, the Renaissance devotional writers experienced mystical encounters with God in the depths of their personal retreat. They strove to escape the entanglements of the world and achieve complete union with Christ, and many of them reported such an experience. We cannot adequately describe their mystical experiences, nor is it within our purpose to evaluate the validity of those experiences. But we should note that the mystical union with Christ reported by Renaissance writers was a central theme of the devotional literature that comes out of this period.

Mysticism is often misunderstood and maligned by sophisticated religious thinkers who believe it is a form of naive emotionalism or, on the other extreme, a kind of incipient demon possession. Neither fear is justified. True mysticism (which the Renaissance devotional writers described more elaborately than any others before or since[2]) is an intimate relationship with Christ in which the worshiper is lifted into ineffably beautiful experiences of communion with his Lord. The intensity of the mystical experience leaves the worshiper incapable of adequately explaining it to others. Yet others can see evidence of it. Thomas Kepler's definition of a saint suggests the evidence common to the mystic and every Christian who consciously lives in the companionship of the living Christ:

"1. His life is saturated with an intense love of the Christian religion as a way of adjusting himself to himself, to his fellow men, and to God. He is a 'religion-intoxicated' person!

"2. He lives with a joyous, radiant, lighthearted freedom, because his life is totally dependent on God....

"3. He emulates Christ in everything he does....

"4. He freely opens his life to God's *agape*—redemptive, free-giving love— and as the recipient of God's *agape* he desires to help the needy, the lost, the unfortunate, the unhappy....

"5. He looks upon Christianity as not merely a theoretical ideal; for him it is a practical way of living with individuals in an unchristian society....

"6. He believes that the Kingdom of God can come into history. But it must continue in him as it began in Christ....

"7. He has a continuous humility....

"8. He looks wistfully into the eyes of every person...as a brother in whom lie the potentialities of a Christian saint.

"9. He is not one desirous of escaping the world through the art of devotion. Rather he is one who becomes stimulated to use the results of worship to better the world....

"10. He is...'a man the light shines through.' "[3]

All of these evidences are significant, but I believe number 9 is usually overlooked, especially in the life of the mystic. We have largely accepted the notion that mystics are "other-worldly" people who live in hermit-like seclusion from the rest of human society. Yet a genuine encounter with Christ prompts just the opposite desire; Christ compels the mystic to be redemptively involved in the world.

Ignatius Loyola was a good example of this. Disgusted by the barbarous behavior he witnessed as a soldier, Loyola retreated to a cave near Manresa, Spain for a year of solitude and contemplation. There he experienced the

[2]Thomas Kepler labels the late medieval and Renaissance era the "Golden Age of Mysticism" in *An Anthology of Devotional Literature* (Grand Rapids: Baker, 1977).
[3]*Ibid.*, pp. 8–9.

sweetness of a mystical relationship with Christ. He left the cave to pursue seven years of university studies in theology, founded the Society of Jesus (the Jesuit order) in France, and became a different kind of soldier for Christ—engaged in the spiritual warfare of Christ's kingdom as energetically as he had been engaged in the military conquests of Spain. Mysticism was for Loyola a this-worldly religious experience. We find a similar emphasis in the writings of other mystics from this period.

What is the value of reading devotional classics from the late medieval and Renaissance period?

Despite the dangers involved with extreme forms of mysticism,[4] the Renaissance mystics challenge us to regain a sense of holy awe. Preoccupied with the daily routine, we are likely to treat lightly our relationship with God; we are prone to view worship with a casual, halfhearted ennui. The Renaissance devotional writers call us to see the Lord "high and lifted up" in his temple of worship. Like Michelangelo and Bernini, who designed soaring basilicas that left Renaissance worshipers agape with wonder, the mystics of this era summon us to abandon our humdrum routine and enter the rapturous experience of wholehearted worship. We are perplexed and sometimes intimidated when we read their work. But we cannot fail to be changed.

Another benefit of the Renaissance devotional writings is that they remind us to strike a healthy balance between corporate, public worship and individual, private worship. We enjoy the fellowship of other Christians. We are enriched by the sharing of corporate worship. Yet by its very nature, corporate worship seldom allows us to submit ourselves to the personal claims of the Lord. In the privacy of individual worship, we hear the prophetic words of God applied to our own lives. We confess our personal failings. We commit ourselves to redemptive change. At the risk of oversimplifying the facts, we might say that corporate worship exalts the Lord while private worship examines the worshiper. That is not strictly true, of course; both kinds of worship involve some elements of divine exaltation and human examination. But generally speaking, the emphasis of each type of worship is different. The Renaissance devotional writers keep clearly before us the importance of private devotion.

IV. Quietism and Pietism (1600—1799)

The divisions of church history we use here are somewhat contrived, because the characteristics of any given era may be found to some degree in the adjoining periods of history. We see that especially in this section, for the in-

---

[4]Gerald Bray cautions: "The mystical experience with God is apophatic, which means that it rejects all human attempts to explain it.... Where [this type of] mysticism has thrived, dogmatic theology has withered, and the two forces have usually been at loggerheads in the course of Church history."—*Creeds, Councils, and Christ* (Downers Grove IL: InterVarsity, 1984), p. 91.

fluences of quietism and pietism were felt long before the seventeenth century; yet they dominated the religious scene at this time.

Quietism is a mode of worship in which the Christian seeks to be totally passive before the Lord, waiting for the impulse of the Holy Spirit to reveal what he should do. Quakers, more conservative Mennonite groups, and a few millennial groups have stressed quietistic religion. Their worship services are unstructured, informal, and meditative—characterized by long periods of silence in which the worshipers "wait for a word from the Lord."

Pietism is another mode of worship that focuses on the redemptive value of keeping the commands of the Lord. Prayer, Bible study, acts of charity, faithful attendance at religious gatherings—these are some activities that pietists believe a Christian should pursue to prove his faithfulness to God. Few would say these activities have any saving merit; but pietists believe such faithful deeds demonstrate the Christian's desire to fulfill all that the Lord requires of him. By persevering in these pious acts, the Christian helps to guard himself from spiritual laxity and backsliding. The Moravians, the Hutterites, the Shakers, and many small pietistic groups which began in the seventeenth and eighteenth centuries continue today. The evangelical revivals led by Whitefield and the Wesleys in the seventeenth century were essentially a pietist movement. Pietism continues to be a shaping influence of modern evangelicalism. So this brief era of church history has great significance for the ongoing character of the Western church.

The world climate was turbulent. Old political systems were being challenged and overthrown. The fall of the monarchy in England and France, the struggle for independence in the American colonies, and the inflammatory political writing of thinkers such as Locke and Voltaire were indicative of the seething cauldron of political change.

Old scientific systems were being likewise challenged and overthrown. These two centuries brought Galileo's astonishing discoveries about the solar system, John Newton's principles of modern physics, William Harvey's breakthroughs in anatomy and medicine, not to mention a wealth of revolutionary finds in other branches of science. These discoveries paved the way for the Industrial Revolution and the modern technological age.

In the religious arena, these two centuries heralded significant change as well. The Protestant Reformation that brought such monumental shakings to the religious houses of Germany, Switzerland, and the British Isles in the 1500s now stagnated as the Reformers took up swords against one another. The Council of Trent (1546) began a Catholic Counter Reformation that reached a flood tide of change in the seventeenth century. Roman Catholic religious orders were reorganized; the Vatican broadened its judicial powers; and the Catholic liturgy was stripped of many of the elaborate accretions of the late medieval age, making it more easily understood and more accessible to the common man. All Christian communions fought to establish a beach-head in the new world—Roman Catholicism carrying the banners of Spain, Portugal, France, and Italy; Anglicans and Puritans under the flag of England; and Russian Orthodox priests manning the bleak arctic colonies of Russia. Their ecclesiastical and doctrinal struggles also became a nationalistic struggle.

Devotional writers encountered new challenges in this era of convulsive change, along with some new versions of the old challenges:

How could they express the Christian faith in terms that made sense to sophisticated thinkers of the Enlightenment as well as to the wild-eyed insurrectionists in the streets? The most highly respected political leaders and publishers were deists. They considered orthodox Christianity to be a monarchial religion, fit to be scuttled along with the scepter of the king. Peasant folk believed the evangelical reformers were too busy with doctrinal fisticuffs to care what happened to the common man. (A notable exception were the circuit-riding preachers of the American frontier; but remember they were the exception rather than the rule, so far as the clerical profile was concerned.)

Further, how could the devotional writers of this era avoid the excesses of mysticism on the one hand and sacramentalism on the other? Either extreme could distort the Christian message; either could divert thousands from Christ at a crucial point in world history.

Oddly, the emergence of modern science did not pose as grave a threat to orthodox Christianity as we commonly believe. Most of the leading scientists of this era were outspoken Christians who said that their discoveries affirmed the truth of Scripture rather than denied it. Johannes Kepler (1571—1630) reveled in his newly discovered principles of astrophysics, by which anyone "can taste in small measure the delight of God, the Supreme Artist....I yield freely to the sacred frenzy...."[5] One might speculate on the different character of science—and of the Christian faith—if more twentieth-century thinkers acknowledged that science and faith affirm the same truth. The conflict between science and religion which we take for granted today did not seem to cross the minds of Baroque thinkers. So natural science and speculative philosophy are curiously absent from the classic Christian writings of that era.

What did concern Christian writers of that age?

First, they emphasized the fact that each Christian possesses the Spirit of God as an "inner light" that enlivens, sustains, and guides. Yet they equally emphasized that God dispenses his saving grace through the ministries of the church. So the "inner light" theme of the quietists did not lead them to privatistic religious practices, as with the Renaissance mystics. Perhaps the quiet-

---

[5]Quoted by Carl Sagan, *Cosmos* (New York: Random House, 1980), p. 64.

ists were aware of those dangers. At any rate, while George Fox, William Law, and others urged their Christian friends to heed the "inner light" of the Spirit, they urged just as insistently that the leadings of the Spirit be submitted to the scrutiny of Scripture and the church.

Second, they emphasized moral and spiritual purity rather than penance. The controversial doctrine of Christian perfection emerged in the quietist/pietist circles at this time. It attracted the idle curiosity of thousands of disillusioned high-church Christians at first; but within a century its explosive force would shatter the perfectionist groups into dozens of smaller sects.

Third, the seventeenth- and eighteenth-century devotional writers encouraged diversity of Christian belief and practice. They recognized that each individual is responsible for progress toward spiritual maturity. Thus they wrote hundreds of tracts and booklets designed to aid the individual's spiritual development. Devotional literature, in the modern sense of that term, originated in these writings.

These Baroque devotional writers employed a couple of new writing genres: the allegory and the devotional commentary. The fanciful stories of allegorical writers such as John Bunyan allowed them to reveal the spiritual faults of their contemporaries in a gentle, entertaining way. This was a marked contrast to the barbed broadsides of Luther, Calvin, and other Reformers. The spiritual allegory was a Christian counterpart to the allegorical plays of Voltaire—both were subtle yet potent forms of social criticism. The other popular genre, the devotional commentary, was not a genuine innovation; Jerome and others had written devotional commentaries before. But after the dogmatic commentaries of Calvin and Luther, the devotional treatments by Matthew Henry, Adam Clarke, Matthew Poole, and their colleagues brought a refreshing popularization of Bible study.

We gain several benefits by reading the devotional writings of these two centuries.

First, the "inner light" theme brings a reassuring, stabilizing effect to Christian experience in times of social upheaval.[6]

Second, our modern age is characterized by a renewed quest for moral and spiritual purity. We see evidence of this in the revival of Wesley studies, for example. Christians are disenchanted with the moral equivocations and theological waywardness of the 1960s and 1970s; they seek a return to the simple standards of pietism. The Baroque writers provide good source material for this renewal of pietism.

---

[6]In this connection, notice that the quietists espoused many ideas similar to those of the "Jesus movement" in the 1960s and 1970s—another movement that flourished in a time of socio-political turmoil.

Most important, the devotional writings of this period parallel today's trend toward an individualistic religion. As mentioned before, the quietist/pietist movement esteemed individual spirituality, yet remained firmly rooted in Scripture and Christian tradition. It managed to avoid the extremes of mysticism and sacramentalism, which could be the twin snares of modern individualistic Christianity.

The devotional writing of this period has special literary value as well. Christian allegorical writing of this period used more overt, easily understood symbols than we find in modern allegories by Lewis, Tolkien, Miller, and others. So the devotional literature of the seventeenth and eighteenth centuries offer us a good opportunity to learn an appreciation for spiritual allegory.

V. Revivalism (1800—1914)

The evangelical revival of the 1760s began a new wave of evangelism and Christian growth that saw the Western church divide into hundreds of tendrils, spreading across the American frontier like a wild vine. This era of revival came to an abrupt end with the start of World War I, which inaugurated a trend toward ecumenism and away from sectarian diversity.

The nineteenth century was a period of rapid expansion and modernization in North America, accompanied by relative calm abroad after the Napoleonic Wars. Historians call the early 1800s the "era of good feeling" because of the prosperity and the general attitude of confidence that characterized the time. The term might be applied to the entire century; at no time before or since has the American mood been so ebullient and hopeful. Christian work flourished in this rich soil of opportunity.

Evangelists used forthright methods for reaching the masses: outdoor preaching, street meetings, tract distribution, newspaper publication of sermons, businessmen's prayer meetings to name a few. American Protestantism suffered wholesale fragmentation into numerous sects, especially during the Civil War. But this did not seem to hinder the spreading influence of evangelical Christianity throughout the growing nation.

Christian leaders needed to communicate spiritual truth to masses of illiterate frontier people who were preoccupied with the basic needs of survival. They had addressed the social ills aggravated by the Industrial Revolution, with its sweatshops and soup lines. They wanted to stress the need for conversion, without disavowing the faith of those who "had always been" Christians.[7] Furthermore, Christian thinkers had to deal with the new liberal schools of biblical interpretations, which left so many troubled and disori-

---

[7]One of the most important books of the nineteenth century was Horace Bushnell's *Christian Nurture,* in which he proposed that someone could be born and grow up as a Christian without needing a crisis conversion experience.

ented pastors in its wake. These were some of the most serious religious challenges of the era.

To meet these challenges, Christian devotional writers shifted toward ever more popular forms of literature such as Christian novels (e.g., Charles Sheldon's *In His Steps*), books of sermons and revival manuals (e.g., Charles Finney's *Revival Lectures*), and inspirational works with a positive cast (such as Hannah Whitall Smith's *Christian's Secret of a Happy Life*). And a popular new genre emerged at the turn of the century: the books of daily devotional readings, such as Mrs. Charles Cowman's *Streams in the Desert* and Oswald Chambers's *My Utmost for His Highest*. All of these books were geared to the casual reader who wanted simple resources for the first steps of spiritual growth.

Thus, the devotional writers of revivalism turned to allegory, religious fiction, and highly visual poetry to express their most profound insights. This was true of devotional writers from the same era who are not normally associated with revivalism as such—the Austrian poet Ranier Marie Rilke, the French novelist Victor Hugo, the American essayist Ralph Waldo Emerson, and the Danish philosopher Soren Kierkegaard are examples. These nineteenth-century Christian writers presented some of their most striking ideas through metaphors and colorful stories that suggested deeper spiritual truths. Apparently, this was not the time to try to sway Christians with abstract thinking. Poetry, yes; philosophy, no.

Some have called this "The Gilded Age" because of Western society's fondness for ornamentation in architecture, furniture, clothing, and daily conversation. One detects a bit of gilding in the devotional writings as well. The style tends to be florid and lushly descriptive; yet some valuable insights shine through.

The turn of the century saw a revival of evangelistic preaching by D. L. Moody, R. A. Torrey, A. B. Simpson, and various evangelists of the holiness movement. In Europe a similar reawakening occurred in the "higher life" conferences where F. B. Meyer, Andrew Murray, and Hannah Whitall Smith were favorite speakers. These revivalists tended to be more forthright in their preaching and their writing, which may help to explain why their devotional works continue to be reprinted while the more gilt-edged Victorian classics are largely forgotten.

VI. The Modern Era (1915—)

World War I brought radical changes to the social and political climate of our world. One may also argue that the "Great War" changed our spiritual climate; perhaps it merely reflected it. World War I revealed the grievous instability of international affairs, the inability of polite traditions to preserve law and order, and the hideous violence that lurked within the heart of the most civilized man. Mustard gas attacks in the trenches of France, bloody massacres in Turkey and Armenia, and anarchists' random bombing of schools and markets in supposedly neutral nations confirmed that the dignified ways of the Gilded Age had not stripped the dark thread of evil from the fabric of the human heart.

In the face of these shocking truths, the flowery musings of nineteenth-century devotional writers soon wilted. Christians now lived in a world where scientific technology gave them the ability to eradicate their enemies by pulling a trigger or pressing a bombadier's button. They could read the mind-probing studies of Sigmund Freud, Carl Jung, and other eminent thinkers of that new science, psychology. They could no longer accept the idyllic notions of the nineteenth-century Christians who thought that education and wealth would usher in an age of universal peace and brotherhood. Man was as savage as ever. The human heart was as desperately wicked as in Noah's day. No Christian could ignore this gruesome fact, and no Christian devotional writer could brush it aside.

So the following years have given us devotional writers who are more likely to deal with the grim realities of war, disease, and irrational violence. The lyrical writers are still with us, of course. But we are more likely to see modern devotional writers deal with themes such as the carnality of man, the irrationality of suffering, and the often perplexing ways of God's will. Even the writers of children's stories are apt to take up these themes, as in *The Lion, the Witch, and the Wardrobe*, by C. S. Lewis. We see it in the whole spectrum of modern devotional works, from fantasy (such as *The Singer Trilogy*, by Calvin Miller) to serious essays (such as *A Severe Mercy*, by Sheldon Van Auken). Culpable human nature and the righteous nature of God are both playing on the stage of our world, and right now the villains seem to have the upper hand. For the most part, modern devotional writers do not try to explain this problem away. They discuss problems such as terminal illness, mass murder, global famine, and thermonuclear war with candor as well as compassion. And they are not afraid to confess that they are sometimes mystified by the way God chooses to act. The mystery of God's ways is a recurrent theme of modern devotional writing; yet the certainty of God's love is just as prevalent in these books.

Inspirational vs. Devotional

The modern press has issued a flood of inspirational books, which should be distinguished from devotional books *per se*. Inspirational books may range over a wide variety of topics, from Bible study to introspective meditation. Some are superficial in their approach, while others show careful thought and artful writing. They are designed to inspire—i.e., to be channels through which God's Holy Spirit can lift and challenge the reader. Because many kinds of books serve this purpose, one is likely to find a variegated mixture of books in the "inspirational" rack of the bookstore, from the Islamic poetry of Kahlil Gibran's *The Prophet* to the romantic allegory of Richard Bach's *Jonathan Livingston Seagull,* with more explicitly Christian books sprinkled among them. "Inspirational" is a subjective term, because the book that uplifts one reader will leave another cold. So the vaguely defined category of inspirational books will continue to grow.

Devotional books, on the other hand, are designed to enhance the reader's personal relationship with Christ by teaching or exemplifying a life of spiritual discipline. While inspirational books may allude to such discipline, they emphasize the results (peace, assurance, spiritual victory) rather than the actual practice of devotion.

This may seem like a contrived distinction, since inspirational books can have genuine value as devotional resources. Yet I think this is a useful distinction, because it underscores the intentional quality of the devotional life. As we noted in Chapter 1, the devotional life is not a kind of pious daydreaming; it is a planned and covenanted meeting with the Lord, in private and public services of worship, to praise him and hear his summons to more faithful service. Most modern inspirational books do not lead us deeper into this intentional way of worship. They share the observations of other Christians (as in the personal testimony books) or exhort us to "get with it" spiritually (as with the positive thinking books). While such books have value, I wish to limit our discussion to books that are explicitly devotional, books that help us fulfill our personal commitment to worship God. We have been blessed by the publication of many good devotional books in this century, and some of them can be expected to stand the test of time to become the devotional classics of the future.

I should briefly mention some specific types of devotional literature that are being revived in this century, examples of which are listed in following chapters:

The journals and prayers of well-known Christians such as Rufus M. Jones, Albert Schweitzer, Anne Morrow Lindbergh, and John Baillie are a vital part of twentieth-century devotional literature. Not only do they express these writers' insights into a worshipful relationship with God, but they encourage other modern Christians by proving that a daily time of prayer and worship is still within their grasp. Most of these books were written by active Christian leaders who traveled widely and carried demanding work assignments; yet these writers made a daily time of private worship a high priority in their lives. See Chapters 7 and 9 for more complete listings of these books.[8]

The twentieth century has produced a number of helpful works on the moral and spiritual demands of Christian living, addressed to the non-Christian or nominally Christian reader. One might call these the modern counterparts of the ante-Nicene apologetics, though these modern works are not as closely reasoned as ancient apologetics. C. S. Lewis's *Mere Christianity,* Dietrich Bonhoeffer's *Cost of Discipleship,* Sundar Singh's *With and Without Christ,* and Ernesto Cardinal's *To Live Is to Love* are examples.

Christian novels and allegories are gaining popularity once again. Many of them, such as the works of Grace Livingston Hill and Janette Oke, are designed largely for entertainment. But a few challenge us to consider the seriousness of our devotion to Christ. See Chapter 6 for more about this type of devotional literature.

This century has given us some fine Christian biographies and autobiographies. Nearly all of these are "inspirational" in the sense I have explained above; but a few choice works such as E. Stanley Jones's *A Song of Ascents,* C. S. Lewis's *Surprised by Joy,* and Thomas Merton's *Seven-Storey Mountain* exemplify various kinds of devotional life worthy of imitation. You will find these modern works listed among other devotional biographies and autobiographies at the end of Chapter 8.

Undiscovered Treasures

Christian publishers and booksellers often hear the complaint, "Why aren't people writing good devotional books anymore?" The fact is, people are writing such books. Careful study of the following bibliography and those of the remaining chapters will reveal that twentieth-century writers are giving us an abundance of good devotional books. We need only to find and use them.

ANNOTATED BIBLIOGRAPHY

Andrewes, Lancelot. *Lancelot Andrewes and His Private Devotions,* Alexander Whyte, ed. Grand Rapids: Baker, 1981.

Andrewes was one of the key translators of the King James Version of the Bible, a man of deep piety and peerless scholarship. This book preserves some of his best meditations of a devotional nature.

Aquinas, Thomas. *Summa Theologica,* 5 vols. Westminster MD: Christian Classics, 1982.

---

[8]Christian song lyrics have blossomed again in the twentieth century, and much of it exhorts the listener to cultivate a devotional life. Such material falls outside the scope of this book; but I would encourage you to consider the emphasis on spirituality in the lyrics of John Michael Talbott and other contemporary musicians.

The greatest philosophical work of the Middle Ages, the *Summa* integrated the existing knowledge of science, theology, and art within the matrix of Aristotelian logic. A sophisticated academic work, the *Summa* nevertheless contains many rich devotional passages. It appeals to the intellectual Christian, yet evidences deep reverence for the revelations of faith.

Augustine. *The City of God*. Garden City NY: Doubleday, n.d.[9]
The African bishop Augustine believed the church was ordained to be the model of God-fearing, morally well-ordered society. "We give the name of the city of God unto that society whereof that Scripture bears witness, which has got the most excellent authority and preeminence of all other works whatsoever..." (x:1). This book exudes the hope that humanity can be transformed through the structure of the sanctified society, namely, the church. It reminds us that spirituality is social. Some medieval readers believed secular society could be made to imitate the *City of God;* that utopian vision never materialized, yet Augustine's book continues to keep before us the practicality of a godly community.

Augustine. *Confessions,* trans. by Edward B. Pusey. New York: Macmillan, 1961.[10]
This frank record of Augustine's spiritual journey, the *Confessions* is comforting to many Christians who feel too inadequate or undisciplined to serve God. The *Confessions* also reveals the strengthening effects of solitude, contemplation, and prayer.

Baxter, Richard. *The Saints' Everlasting Rest*. Grand Rapids: Baker, n.d.
Though he was a leading minister of the Church of England, serving for some time as chaplain to the king, Baxter favored the pietistic ideas of the Puritans. He wrote several books that encouraged his followers to pursue a more obedient and godly life. This is his best-known devotional work. It explains how Christians can better enjoy the blessings of God if they devote themselves to worship, Bible study, and Christian service.

Berdyaev, Nikolai A. *Solitude and Society,* trans. by George Reavey. Westport CT: Greenwood Press, 1976.
Berdyaev was expelled from Russia in 1922 because of his staunch commitment to Christ. He later became director of the Academy of the Philosophy of

---

[9]Also available from Penguin (New York, 1984) and Modern Library (New York, 1950).
[10]Also available in a translation by R. S. Pine-Coffin (New York: Penguin, 1961); by Rex Warner (New York: New American Library, n.d.); (Doubleday, Garden City NY n.d.); and Moody (Chicago, 1984). It is also available as *The Confessions of Augustine*, W. R. Connor and John Gibbs, editors (Salem NY: Ayer Co., 1979) and as an abridged edition entitled *The Confessions of St. Augustine* (Grand Rapids: Baker, 1977).

Religion in Paris. Berdyaev is best known for his philosophical writings, but *Solitude and Society* concerns a crucial issue of the devotional life—the way in which societal man is most authentically human, as opposed to the person who lives in isolation. Berdyaev discusses the benefits of solitary worship, yet concludes that man can be most fully "spiritual" as he lives with others.

Bernard of Clairvaux. *On Loving God,* ed. by Hugh Martin. Westport CT: Greenwood Press, 1981.

Bernard has earned a permanent place in church history for bringing reform to the monastic movement at a crucial point in the medieval era. Bernard's hymns and letters have been cherished by Christian leaders of all ages, including John Calvin and Martin Luther. *On Loving God* brings together devotional selections from Bernard's sermons.

Buttrick, George A. *Prayer.* Nashville: Abingdon, 1948.

This is a practical manual on the life of prayer, written by a leading Presbyterian minister of the twentieth century. Buttrick gives clear counsel about the purpose and practice of prayer. The insights of his book can be readily understood and implemented by any layperson.

Calvin, John. *The Piety of John Calvin,* trans. by Ford L. Battles, Stanley Tagg, ed. Grand Rapids: Baker, 1977.

An excellent compilation of the devotional writings of this great Reformer. Calvin is best known for his theological writings, especially his *Institutes of the Christian Religion.* But he also dealt with prayer, meditation, fasting, and many other devotional concerns; Battles's anthology brings those writings together for the first time.

Christensen, Bernhard M., ed. *The Inward Pilgrimage: Spiritual Classics from Augustine to Bonhoeffer.* Minneapolis: Augsburg, 1975.

If you are intrigued by the idea of reading the devotional classics but do not know where to start, Christensen gives you a sample of some of the best devotional works from every era of church history. Augustine, Luther, Bunyan, and other devotional masters are represented in this fine collection.

Edwards, Jonathan. *A Treatise on Religious Affections.* Grand Rapids: Baker, 1982.[11]

We remember Jonathan Edwards as a great Calvinist preacher and a bold

---

[11]Also available as volume 2 of *The Works of Jonathan Edwards,* edited by John E. Smith (New Haven CT: Yale University Press, 1959), and edited by James M. Houston (Portland OR: Multnomah, 1984).

leader of the American colonists. Yet he left us some treasured devotional writings as well. This book discusses the interplay of human will and emotions as a person seeks to serve God. Edwards considers the qualities that mark the life of a "spiritual" person, compared to others. This is a reserved and dignified book, full of Edwards's colonial "starch"; yet it provides some enduring insights into the character of a devout Christian.

Fenélon, Francois de. *Spiritual Letters to Women.* New Canaan CT: Keats, 1980.[12]

From his position as Archbishop of Cambrai, Fenelon counseled many wealthy families of France during the late seventeenth and early eighteenth centuries. In this collection of Fenélon's letters to ladies, he advises humility, simplicity, and quietness before God. Fenélon was a good friend of Madame Guyon, a leader of the French quietists.

Francis de Sales. *Introduction to the Devout Life.* Nashville: The Upper Room, n.d.

Written for Christians who yearn to have a deep devotional life in the midst of their busy daily routine, this book deals with emotional as well as spiritual conflicts that the Christian can expect. Francis de Sales served as bishop of Geneva and adamantly contested John Calvin's Protestant ideas. Yet today Protestants as well as Roman Catholics recognize him as a man of deep spiritual insight.

Francis of Assisi. *The Little Flowers of St. Francis,* trans. by Raphael Brown. Garden City NY: Doubleday, 1958.

This collection of stories, sermons, and hymns conveys the personal warmth of Francis and his sense of being at one with all of God's creation. Protestants will be disturbed by some of the events related in *The Little Flowers* (e.g., Francis's sermon to the birds and the appearance of stigmata in his hands), and any objective reader will recognize that a fair amount of Franciscan myth is interwoven with the facts. Nevertheless the book reveals much of the devotional spirit of this great saint.

Gregory Palamas. *The Triads,* trans. by Nicholas Gendle. New York: Paulist Press, 1983.

Early Eastern Orthodox monks were powerfully influenced by Platonism, which led them to try to escape their physical bodies through mystical experiences of God because they thought the body was evil and repugnant to God. Origen, Evagrius, and other Eastern devotional writers urged their followers

---

[12]Also published by Zondervan, (Grand Rapids, 1984).

to unite their minds with God's mind through various ascetical exercises. Palamas argued for a spirituality that acknowledged man's physical limits, yet found contentment through prayerful communion with Christ. His three-volume defense of this biblically sound, realistic devotional life, commonly called *the Triads,* marks an important watershed in Eastern Orthodox spirituality. It was written in the fourteenth century.

Herman, Nicholas, ["Brother Lawrence"]. *The Practice of the Presence of God.* Westwood NJ: Fleming H. Revell, 1958.[13]
Serving as a kitchen worker in the monastery of Discalced Carmelites in Paris, Brother Lawrence resented other monks who had time for prayer and contemplation. Then he realized that God was with him in every daily task, even his menial kitchen chores, so he decided to acknowledge and respect God's presence through very simple acts of listening and obedience. This simple book encourages all busy Christians to acknowledge God in the midst of their daily routine.

Ignatius of Loyola. *Spiritual Exercises,* trans. by Anthony Mattola. Garden City NY: Doubleday, n.d.[14]
Ignatius founded the Society of Jesus (commonly known as the Jesuits) to be a disciplined cadre of religious men who would do the pope's bidding, like a holy army ready for combat. He wrote the *Spiritual Exercises* as a manual of discipline to help these men develop a fuller devotional life. Many Christians have benefited from the simple, no-nonsense instruction of the *Exercises.*

John of the Cross. *The Collected Works of St. John of the Cross,* trans. by Kieran Kavanaugh and Otilio Rodriguez. Washington DC: ICS Publications, 1973.[15]
John of the Cross brought a more austere mood to the Carmelite monastic order of Spain and called Roman Catholic contemplatives back to a lifestyle of simplicity at a time (sixteenth century) when materialism seemed to be invading the monastery itself. Kepler finds in him "a sensitive spirit deeply influenced by all that was lovely and attractive" (p. 284). This collection includes his best-known work, *The Dark Night of the Soul,* as well as his more deeply mystical works such as *The Ascent of Mount Carmel* and *The Living Flame of Love.*

Kelly, Thomas R. *A Testament of Devotion.* New York: Harper and Row, 1941.

---

[13]Also available in a modernized version edited by Donald E. Demaray (Grand Rapids: Baker, 1975).
[14]Also available in several modernized treatments. See bibliography for Chapter 1.
[15]*Dark Night of the Soul* is available separately in a translation by Benedict Zimmerman from Attic Press, (Greenwood SC, 1974).

Rufus M. Jones said, "Here is a book I can recommend along with the best of the ancient ones." Kelly writes out of his Quaker experience of meditation and prayer. He counsels us to cultivate an awareness of God's light and power through "mental habits of inward orientation." This is one of the best twentieth-century devotional books, surely destined to be recognized as a classic.

Kepler, Thomas S. *An Anthology of Devotional Literature.* Grand Rapids: Baker, 1977.

I referred to this volume often in preparing the present *Resource Guide*, and so I am pleased to see that Baker has reprinted it. Kepler gives a biographical sketch of each devotional writer represented in the volume, with at least one excerpt (often three or more) from that writer's best work. A massive volume, it might be more accurately called a reference book than an anthology; I imagine one would pull it from the shelf to read a selection now and then, rather than trying to read them all consecutively.

Law, William. *A Serious Call to a Devout and Holy Life.* Philadelphia: Westminster, 1968.[16]

First published in 1728, *A Serious Call* stimulated the conscience of John Wesley, George Whitefield, and a host of other evangelical leaders. English essayist Samuel Johnson felt deeply convicted after reading it. *A Serious Call* examines the ungodly lifestyles of various classes of people and holds forth the ideal of a life of Christian holiness. *A Serious Call* still stings the consciences of people who are willing to examine their lives.

Maloney, George A., ed. *Pilgrimage of the Heart.* New York: Harper and Row, 1983.

Here are choice selections from the hard-to-find classics of the Eastern church. Maloney has gathered a set of essays, homilies, and letters that well express the spirit of Eastern Orthodox mysticism.

Murray, Andrew. *The Inner Chamber.* Fort Washington PA: Christian Literature Crusade, n.d.

Millions have been blessed by the inspirational books of Andrew Murray, a saintly pastor who ministered in South Africa at the turn of the century. *The Inner Chamber* emphasizes the importance of having a daily quiet time with God. It suggests some methods of preparing oneself, spiritually and mentally, for that devotional time.

---

[16]Also available from Morehouse, (Wilton CT, 1982); and in condensed form as volume 1 of *The Heart of True Spirituality: John Wesley's Own Choice,* edited by Frank Baker (Grand Rapids: Zondervan, 1985).

Otto, Rudolf. *The Idea of the Holy,* trans. by John W. Harvey, 2nd ed. New York: Oxford University Press, 1950.

One of the great German devotional writers of this century, Rudolf Otto was a revered professor of philosophy at Marburg. *The Idea of the Holy* is his most enduring work. It contrasts the mysterious and majestic presence of God with the searching spirit of man. Though Otto uses the language of a philosopher and theologian, his work bears the mark of genuine spirituality and reverence for the experience of worship.

Pascal, Blaise. *Penséės,* trans. by A. J. Krailsheimer. New York: Penguin, 1966.[17]

The seventeenth-century philosopher and mathematician Blaise Pascal had a profound conversion experience at the age of thirty-one. This led him to begin writing his magnificent *Penséės (Thoughts),* which remained unfinished at his death. These collected essays reveal the ironies of Pascal's life—a man of sophisticated logic overwhelmed by his personal encounters with God. So the book variously moves through the realms of philosophy and mysticism, creating a novel amalgam of faith and reason.

Simpson, A. B. *The Life of Prayer.* Camp Hill PA: Christian Publications, n.d.

A. B. Simpson was a Presbyterian minister who experienced a spiritual reawakening that led him to start a new urban ministry in Brooklyn, New York, at the turn of the century. His work later became the Christian and Missionary Alliance. Simpson is widely respected as a key devotional writer of the holiness movement. This book details his insights into the methods of effectual prayer. It is written in a simple, popular style.

Taylor, Jeremy. *Holy Living.* New York: Harper and Row, 1971.[18]

This abridged edition serves up the spiritual meat of Taylor's 1650 devotional classic, which greatly influenced the Wesleys and other leaders of the eighteenth-century evangelical revival. Taylor calls for more disciplined Christian living, based on simple obedience to God's Word.

Teresa of Avila. *The Way of Perfection,* trans. by E. Allison Peers. Garden City NY: Doubleday, 1964.

Though best known for her mystical writings, Teresa was also capable of giving practical instruction in the cultivation of a life of devotion. This seems

---

[17]Also available under the title, *The Thoughts of Blaise Pascal* (Westport CT: Greenwood Press, 1978).

[18]Also available from Century Bookbindery (Philadelphia PA, 1982) and Morehouse (Wilton CT, 1982).

to be her most accessible work. She explains that love for others, detachment from materialism, and a humble attitude toward God and one's fellow man are the prerequisites of genuine prayer.

Thomas à Kempis. *The Imitation of Christ,* trans. by E. M. Blaiklock. Nashville: Thomas Nelson, 1981.[19]

An Augustinian monk, Thomas á Kempis edited and published this spiritual diary of a Dutch preacher named Gerhard Groot in 1441. The book is a series of pithy aphorisms that challenge us to imitate the spirit and mind of our Lord. The book is available in translations and condensed editions too numerous to list here.

Watchman Nee. *The Normal Christian Life.* Fort Washington PA: Christian Literature Crusade, 1963.[20]

Watchman Nee was one of the most outspoken evangelical leaders of China, establishing some two hundred churches before he was imprisoned by the Communists in 1950. *The Normal Christian Life* delves into several rich New Testament passages that describe a Christian's daily relationship with his Lord and the spiritual disciplines a Christian must exercise to maintain that relationship. A study guide for this book is also available.

---

[19]Also available in various translations and editions from Carillon Books (St. Paul MN, 1977), Moody (Chicago, 1980), Penguin (New York, 1952), Templegate (Springfield IL, 1980), Morehouse (Wilton CT, 1982), Paraclete Press (Orleans MA, 1982), Zondervan (Grand Rapids, 1983), Doubleday (Garden City NY, 1976), and in a large-print edition from Keats (New Canaan CT, 1982).
[20]Also available from Tyndale House, (Wheaton IL, 1977).

Chapter Three
Inspirational Books

The twentieth century might be called the era of the inspirational book. By far the majority of books now being published by Christian presses are of this type—books that uplift and encourage the Christian by sharing the authors' personal experiences, reflections upon Scripture, and musings about the challenges of the Christian life. These books do not give detailed instruction in the methods of devotional worship, but they describe the results of a vital relationship with the Lord. So I think they deserve a place in our discussion of devotional resources.

Who can say when inspirational books were first written?

Perhaps the New Testament epistles were the first inspirational writings to be published; they certainly were designed to uplift and encourage the Christians to whom they were addressed. The Gospels and the Book of Revelation did the same. And if we were to trace the subsequent history of Christian literature, we surely would find rich inspirational writings in every age. They appear as letters, homilies, tracts, and books; but in whatever form, they have comforted and emboldened the hearts of millions.

When the pressures of living became most acute, the refreshing springs of devotional literature burst forth more abundantly than ever. Perhaps that explains why inspirational books are so plentiful in our own day. We need comfort, assurance, and hope in the midst of these difficult times. Inspirational books share what other Christians have learned in grappling with problems like ours; they allow us to view troublesome circumstances from a vantage point of faith.

Radio commentator Earl Nightingale is fond of saying, "We become what we think about." It's true. The ideas that we mull over will become the pattern of our personality. We will assume new attitudes, embrace new convictions, and set new goals for life based on the things we choose to think about each day. There is a further application of this principle in the Christian's spiritual life: We become what we think about and what we read about. The books we choose to read will frame the walls of the spiritual "house" we are building. Carole Mayhall has pictured this most helpfully:

> The foundation of our house is Christ, the roof is His love, and the walls are the
> Word of God, prayer, obedience, fellowshipping with other Christians, witness-

ing.... If we lay a foundation and then fail to build the walls, it is like building a foundation for a house and then finding garbage all over the foundation and spending the day cleaning up the garbage. The next day the wind has blown leaves all over the foundation so that we work at sweeping off the leaves. The following week it snows and we diligently shovel off the snow....[1]

Without the "walls" of spiritual discipline, we never get on with the task of building for Christ. Devotional books tell us how to build, but inspirational books tell us how the building should look. Both furnish the raw material of our spiritual house, be it sticks and stubble—or bricks, mortar, and iron. What sort of Christian books are you reading now? They will help to determine the kind of person you become. Inspirational books can provide resilient material for the building of your life.

In the bibliography that follows, I have attempted to list the most helpful inspirational books currently in print. This is by far the longest listing of resources in the *Resource Guide,* yet hundreds of inspirational books are not included. I advise you to select an inspirational book with as much care as you would give to the selection of an expensive Bible reference book, because you will become what you think about—and what you read. Here are some characteristics you should seek as you select inspirational books for your devotional study:

1. The centrality of Christ. How does the inspirational book describe Jesus? How important is the lordship of Christ to the book's overall message?

Too many inspirational books focus on human emotions rather than on Christ. They are nothing more than essays in pop psychology, with a thin veneer of churchly language. Avoid such books. They will impoverish your soul.

A truly inspiring Christian book will evidence a sense of reverence for the Lord Jesus. It will bear the marks of the author's own intimate relationship with the Lord. It will cause us to crave that sort of relationship with Jesus too.

2. The authority of Scripture. How does the author refer to Scripture? as a reference to lend weight to his own claims as a comforting symbol of tradition?

Or does the writer look to Scripture as the chief source of spiritual insight? Does the book flow out of earnest Bible study? Does it bear the marks of genuine reverence for the written Word?

I believe we are tempted to make our devotional life a law unto itself. We are tempted to let exhilarating experiences validate what we think and do. But we must test our Christian experience by the standard of God's Word. As the psalmist was seeking a deeper spiritual experience, he confessed to the Lord,

---

[1]Carole Mayhall, *Lord, Teach Me Wisdom* (Colorado Springs: NavPress, 1979), pp. 167–168.

"Thy word is a lamp unto my feet and a light to my path" (Psa. 119:105). Such an attitude should permeate our devotional experience, and it should permeate the books we read as devotional resources. A respect for the authority of the Word will save us from grievous errors.

3. Realism about the human condition. Some recent inspirational books have a starry-eyed idealism about human nature. The writers assume that if we are spiritually mature and free of unconfessed sin, we will have lives of unfettered victory and power. They relate episodes of miraculous healing, broken habits, relieved depression, and overwhelming joy as if they were the normal pattern of a Christian's daily life. If only that were so! But the man or woman of God knows suffering, grief, and depression in the midst of a proper relationship with God. In fact, these seem to be forms of the "refiner's fire" that God uses to purify and strengthen our souls. An inspirational book should recognize these things are just as normal in the Christian's life as the pleasant aspects of victory, joy, and peace.

Dr. Melvin E. Dieter of Asbury Theological Seminary once showed me photostatic copies of the journals of Hannah Whitall Smith, author of *The Christian's Secret of a Happy Life.* While studying Mrs. Smith's journals, Dr. Dieter found long periods of depression—bordering on despair—when she felt utterly abandoned by God. "One usually thinks of *The Christian's Secret* as a positive, upbeat book," Dr. Dieter said. "But after reading Hannah's journals, I went back to read her classic book, and I began to see an undercurrent of pain beneath her happy words." I think an inspirational book should have that sort of human realism if it is to give us any long-lasting spiritual benefit. Perhaps we cannot detect it on the first reading; but it should have that underlying honesty about our human frailty. Only then can we believe the book's good news is true.

4. Practical in everyday life. As we saw in Chapter 2, many devotional books of the medieval era were written by people living in cloisters, yet they gave their readers methods that could be used in daily life anywhere. This should be true of any devotional book. I believe it also should be true of any inspirational book; it should demonstrate that a life of deep spirituality can be lived anytime, anywhere, not just in seclusion.

This is one of the glaring weaknesses of the inspirational books written by modern Hindus and Buddhists. They espouse a very secluded, individualistic kind of spirituality, yet few people can enjoy long periods of privacy or isolation. Besides, if closet religion is the only true religion, one wonders why some of the most dynamic religious leaders emerged in communities (Quaker, Mennonite, Puritan), where spirituality was clearly a social process. I leave this question to the sociologists of religion. But the fact remains: Very devout people have experienced their spiritual growth in the jostle of everyday life, as they mingled and interacted with all sorts of other people. Jesus' twelve disciples grew in this way. So did the Spirit-filled church in Jerusalem: the Holy Spirit came upon them in private (Acts 2), but he compelled them to live and learn their faith in the streets.

So I am very hesitant to recommend an inspirational book that extolls the joys of solitary Christianity, or academic Christianity, or any other form that is not typical of the everyday life of common people. The Bible portrays a practical faith, a faith that works in real-life situations. That's the sort of faith I expect to read about when I open an inspirational book.

5. Acknowledging the supernatural. We live in a scientific age when most people are skeptical of supernatural events. Granted, science is a valuable tool for understanding and coping with our environment; yet God often acts in ways that defy scientific explanation. An inspirational book must acknowledge the mystery—yes, the irrationality—that may color the Christian's life, or it is not being true to the character of Christian experience.

For example, how shall we explain Jesus' raising of Lazarus from the dead? or Paul's surviving a poisonous snakebite? or the amazing recovery of thousands of hospital patients who have been given up for dead?

How shall we explain the sudden clearing of the minds of demented persons in response to Jesus? or the Christian conversion of Emperor Constantine? or the dramatic about-face of a Blaise Pascal, a Leo Tolstoy, or a Malcolm Muggeridge?

We cannot put God in a box of neat logical propositions. We cannot analyze the mind of God with the cold logic of a clinician. So an inspirational book that attempts to give pat explanations of what God thinks and how God acts is not telling the whole story. Indeed, I wonder whether the author personally knows the Christian experience about which he is writing; I doubt that anyone who has dealt with God any length of time could honestly say that God's ways are neatly predictable. God's ways are marked by mystery, surprise, and awestruck wonder.

An inspirational book that records genuine Christian experience will acknowledge the wonder of God. It will confess how much the author does not understand about God, along with what he does.

After reading these five characteristics of a sound inspirational book, you may doubt whether there could be a list of books that measure up to these standards. The books in the bibliography on page 60 seem to meet the criteria. You surely will think of other inspirational books that have been channels of God's blessing to your life which you would add to the list.

Because of the vast quantity of inspirational books now available, this list is by no means exhaustive. But it is representative of the fine inspirational books that depict an authentic Christian life. Perhaps some of these books will lead to renewal in your own Christian life; if so, they will have served their most vital purpose as devotional resources.

ANNOTATED BIBLIOGRAPHY

Allen, Charles L. *God's Psychiatry.* Old Tappan NJ: Fleming H. Revell, 1978.[2]

Thousands of Christians have found reassurance and good counsel through this little book. Dr. Allen, a noted United Methodist pastor, takes us on a pastoral study of the Twenty-Third Psalm, the Ten Commandments, the Beatitudes, and the Lord's Prayer. In each of these monumental Scripture texts, Dr. Allen points out a clear Bible teaching to help us find stability in the midst of emotional stress. An excellent gift for troubled persons.

Allen, Charles L. *Perfect Peace.* Old Tappan NJ: Fleming H. Revell, 1979.

One might best call this a therapeutic book. Clearly, Pastor Allen intended these meditations to help confused and disconsolate people find God's power for rebuilding their lives. Allen shares many incidents from his pastoral experience to show how broken lives can be restored to wholeness through a deep relationship with God.

Arthur, Kay. *How Can I Live?* Old Tappan NJ: Fleming H. Revell, 1981.

Kay Arthur hosts a popular series of Bible study seminars, especially for women's groups. She has assisted thousands of Christians in learning how to apply the truth of the Bible to everyday needs. In this book, she leads us through a daily study of Scripture with an emphasis on real-life applications. Each month centers on a given theme; yet the reader will encounter a great variety of issues in a year's time with this "nuts and bolts" devotional study.

Bailey, Keith M. *The Children's Bread.* Camp Hill PA: Christian Publications, 1977.

One of the best modern books on divine healing, Bailey's work shows that God grants healing as part of the promise to his church. The book investigates how to pray for healing, how to remove obstacles to healing, and what to do if we are not healed.

Berquist, Maurice. *The Miracle and Power of Blessing.* Anderson IN: Warner Press, 1982.

This book addresses the same theme as Myron C. Madden's *The Power to Bless* (see below). Though not as careful in its examination of Scripture and sometimes a bit ambiguous in its statements, this book contains some interesting anecdotes and quotations from other Christian authors that supplement Madden's work.

---

[2]Also available from Jove Publications (New York, 1984).

Bilheimer, Robert S. *A Spirituality for the Long Haul.* Philadelphia: Fortress, 1984.

Rejecting the superficial, sentimental devotional patterns that many Christians seem to prefer, Bilheimer examines what Scripture says should be the model for Christian spirituality. His book is more intellectually sophisticated than most of the works I have listed here; but I believe it will serve the needs of Christians who seek a spirituality that is well reasoned as well as warmly experienced.

Birkey, Vera. *You Are Very Special: A Biblical Guide to Self-Worth.* Old Tappan NJ: Fleming H. Revell, 1977.

Each woman would enjoy this exploration of how to reflect upon her own life—with its opportunities, obstacles, and God-ordained gifts—and appreciate the unique person God made her to be. A very affirming book for women who feel inadequate or neglected by God.

Bolding, Amy. *Easy Devotions to Give.* Grand Rapids: Baker, 1981.

Throughout the *Resource Guide,* we have discussed "devotional" primarily in the sense of an individual's private time of worship. But at times one is asked to "give a devotion" for a group—i.e., a brief inspirational thought that will guide the group into a time of worship. Amy Bolding, a retired pastor's wife, has compiled several books of these short devotional talks. Each selection in this volume is based on a familiar Scripture text but has a "catchy" title to arouse interest.

Bolding, Amy. *Fingertip Devotions.* Grand Rapids: Baker, 1970.

Like her other books, Mrs. Bolding's *Fingertip Devotions* contains brief talks that may be given in public meetings to open a period of worship. These selections are ready to use as they are, "at your fingertips."

Bonhoeffer, Dietrich.   *The Cost of Discipleship.* New York: Macmillan, 1949.[3]

Bonhoeffer was one of the few evangelical German pastors who publicly condemned Hitler's policies during World War II. Charged with treason, he spent much of the war in jail and was hanged just before the Allies liberated his sector. In this book, Bonhoeffer condemns the tendency of modern Christians to want "cheap grace"—i.e., a relationship with God that costs the disciple very little. Bonhoeffer argues that God requires costly obedience from every Christian, a lesson well illustrated by Pastor Bonhoeffer's own experience. Though more theologically sophisticated than most inspirational books,

---

[3]Also available from Peter Smith Publishers, Inc. (Magnolia MA, 1983).

The Cost of Discipleship is a genuine classic.

Bonhoeffer, Dietrich. *Psalms: The Prayer Book of the Bible,* trans. by James Burtness. Minneapolis: Augsburg, 1970.

An excellent inspirational study of the Psalms, this short book teaches us how to use the praise and worship of these Scriptures to orient our own times of worship. If you are acquainted only with Bonhoeffer's intellectual genius, this book will introduce you to his warm spirituality.

Brandt, Henry R. *The Struggle for Inner Peace.* Wheaton IL: Victor Books, 1984.

Restlessness, dissatisfaction, and anxiety grip the hearts of modern Christians. Peace of mind seems an unattainable ideal. Yet this Christian psychologist shows that peace is a norm of the Christian life. He explains how troubled Christians can obtain peace, not through more striving, but through realizing where they stand with the Lord.

Brooks, D. P. *Free to Be Christian.* Nashville: Broadman, 1981.

Brooks applies Scripture teaching about the liberating power of Jesus Christ to the hang-ups that modern Christians typically experience. He shows that Jesus calls us to be growing, forward-tending people who are not hemmed by our old habits, traditions, or biased opinions.

Calvin, John. *Golden Booklet of the True Christian Life.* Grand Rapids: Baker, 1975.

In a handy size that can be carried in briefcase or purse, this extract from Calvin's devotional writings may revive an interest in the spirituality of this leading theologian. The *Golden Booklet* highlights some of Calvin's most helpful comments on prayer and the process of Christian growth.

Carmichael, Amy. *Candles in the Dark.* Fort Washington PA: Christian Literature Crusade, 1982.

This inspiring little book was extracted from the letters that Carmichael wrote during her last illness, which confined her to a solitary room in her mission compound at Dohnavur, India. She writes candidly and reverently about her relationship with the Lord during this long seige of suffering. This book is sure to encourage others who must endure pain for protracted periods of time.

Carretto, Carlo. *Letters from the Desert,* trans. by Rose Mary Hancock. Maryknoll NY: Orbis Books, 1972.[4]

Carlo Carretto was a political activist for the Vatican during the turbulent

---

[4]Also available from Jove Publications (New York, 1976).

years surrounding World War II. But in the 1950s he went to Algeria to join a group of contemplative monks and try to learn how to pray once again. He wrote this brief account of what happened to explain to his friends why he chose to remain in the desert rather than return to the cloak-and- dagger world of Italian politics. One discerns a close similarity between Carretto's experience and that of the Desert Fathers centuries ago. He urges us to learn the joys of solitude and contemplation, even if we cannot go to the desert to find them.

Christenson, Evelyn. *Lord, Change Me!* Wheaton IL: Victor Books, 1977.

Mrs. Christenson had prayed long for her husband to change some habits and attitudes that irked her and strained the harmony of their marriage. Then God revealed that she needed to change. That experience gave her a new understanding of the purpose of prayer—that it brings the pray-er into conformity to God's will, rather than vice versa. She shares vivid and often funny incidents from her prayer retreats, in which women have had their lives realigned to God through prayer.

Christenson, Evelyn. *What Happens When Women Pray.* Wheaton IL: Victor Books, 1975.

Having led scores of prayer retreats and weekday prayer groups, Mrs. Christenson marvels at the great power that she has seen unlocked by prayer. Her book brims over with victorious episodes in which a few women persisted in prayer. A good book for group study as well as your individual reading.

Clark, Glenn. *I Will Lift Up Mine Eyes.* San Francisco: Harper and Row, 1984.

This book is a unique mixture of the inspirational and practical considerations of devotional life. Clark gives us a twenty-eight-day self-directed course in prayer, complete with exercises that allow us to develop a variety of prayer methods. But much of the book concerns the results of a vital prayer life—how it will affect our relationships with other human beings as well as our relationship with God.

Clarkson, Margaret. *Destined for Glory: The Meaning of Suffering.* Grand Rapids: Eerdmans, 1983.

Reflecting on her lifelong struggle with pain, the author tells how she came to accept it as part of God's sovereign plan for life. Some will not agree with her theological ideas, but anyone who has suffered will find something in common with her effort to make sense of the ordeal.

Coleman, Robert E. *Songs of Heaven.* Old Tappan NJ: Fleming H. Revell, 1982.

Most Christians read the Book of Revelation for its predictions; but Dr. Coleman has read it for its praise. This unusual little book lifts up several passages from Revelation that exalt the Lord Jesus Christ. Coleman explains how to use these praise songs in our own devotional worship.

Conwell, Russell H. *Acres of Diamonds.* New York: Harper and Row, 1915.[5]

Dr. Conwell spent much of his later years traveling across the United States to deliver this lecture in churches, college halls, and everywhere he could find a hearing. He underscores the sad failure of many Christians who neglect the great resources God has given them. Rather than expending our lives in the pursuit of material riches through our own fanatical effort or scheming, we should open our eyes to the riches of God's kingdom that already lie within our grasp. A challenging little book.

Dalrymple, John. *Living the Richness of the Cross.* Notre Dame IN: Ave Maria, 1983.

Dalrymple is a Roman Catholic priest in Edinburgh, Scotland and a noted retreat leader. In this book he explains how a Christian in suffering finds spiritual strength from the suffering Christ. Despite the profundity of this theme, Dalrymple avoids pious speculation or abstract theologizing, to present instead a clear and meaningful set of meditations on the spiritual side of suffering.

Day, Gwynn M. *Joy Beyond.* Grand Rapids: Baker, 1979.

These meditations on heaven are especially good for the bereaved or those facing imminent death. Each selection draws our attention to a Bible promise concerning eternal life.

Drakeford, John W. *The Awesome Power of the Healing Thought.* Nashville: Broadman, 1981.

Dr. Drakeford, a professor at Southwestern Baptist Theological Seminary, explains how our thoughts affect our physical health—so much so that we must have the right thoughts and attitudes in order to be healed. His book points to an often neglected facet of the Christian's devotional life, the interrelationship of the spiritual and the physical.

Drummond, Henry. *The Greatest Thing in the World.* Old Tappan NJ: Fleming H. Revell, 1968.[6]

---

[5]Also available from Fleming H. Revell (Old Tappan NJ, 1975) and Jove Publications (New York, 1982).

[6]Also available from Putnam Publishing Group (New York, 1959), Brownlow Publishing Co. (Fort Worth, TX, 1981), and Whitaker House, (Springdale PA, 1981).

A Scottish minister who often toured the United States, Drummond gave this inspiring lecture on the Bible's "love chapter," 1 Corinthians 13. He considers each of the personal characteristics of someone who loves with this authentic, God-inspired love. And he concludes that every human relationship could be transformed by the redemptive power of this love. This is a beautifully written little book, just as relevant to our lives today as it was to our great-grandparents.

Drummond, Lewis A. *The Revived Life*. Nashville: Broadman, 1982.
Drummond explains how a Christian's life can be revived to full spiritual vitality through a fresh enduement with the Holy Spirit. He gives case studies of several well-known Christians who have experienced this new empowerment in their own lives.

Eastman, Dick. *A Celebration of Praise*. Grand Rapids: Baker, 1984.
Eastman's earlier books (*The Hour That Changed the World* and *No Easy Road*) have dealt with the general aspects of prayer; this new volume concentrates on the aspect of praise. Eastman explains that praise is concerned with the nature and character of God himself: Not what he does, but who he is. The author then proposes a seven-week "praise strategy" for learning how to offer exultant praise to God.

Eastman, Dick. *No Easy Road*. Grand Rapids: Baker, 1973.
Eastman calls daily prayer "the hour that changes the world," and he has begun a ministry of leading seminars on prayer known as the "Change the World School of Prayer." In this slender volume, Eastman reminds us that fruitful prayer does not just happen; it is the result of disciplined, persistent devotion on our part.

Elliff, Thomas D. *Praying for Others*. Nashville: Broadman, 1979.
Intercessory prayer—praying for others—is a privilege and duty of every Christian. Yet we often wonder how to pray for a certain need, when to pray, and what to expect in answer. Elliff has made a careful study of what Scripture teaches on intercessory prayer and shares the experiences of some modern Christians who have applied these teachings in their own prayer life.

Emurian, Ernest K. *Famous Stories of Inspiring Hymns*. Grand Rapids: Baker, 1975.
Music is a medium that God often uses to inspire our hearts and call us to more consecrated Christian service. Emurian traces the stories of how some of our favorite hymns were written, stories which are often as inspiring as the hymns themselves. The book is also appropriate as a group worship resource

where a story might be used to introduce a hymn that the worshipers will sing. But I think it has great inspirational value for private devotions as well.

Getz, Gene. *Encouraging One Another.* Wheaton IL: Victor Books, 1981.

Using the life of Barnabas as a model, Getz explores a variety of ways in which Christians can build up one another's faith. This makes an excellent group study.

Gordon, Arthur. *A Touch of Wonder.* Old Tappan NJ: Fleming H. Revell, 1976.

Clearly the most popular book by this cherished inspirational author, *A Touch of Wonder* suggests the attitudes and habits that allow us to be more aware of God's blessings each day. Simply written, yet the fruit of deep meditation on the art of Christian living.

Gordon, S. D. *Quiet Talks on Prayer.* Grand Rapids: Baker, 1980.

We might have listed this book in the bibliography for Chapter 7 since Gordon offers much practical advice on the methods of prayer. Yet the pervasive mood of the book is inspirational. He wishes to show that prayer is vital to deepening our communion with the Lord.

Gordon, S. D. *Quiet Talks on Service.* Grand Rapids: Baker, 1980.

Another volume in Gordon's popular "Quiet Talks" series, this book considers how intimate communion with Christ is essential to any form of Christian service. Gordon shows the intrinsic bond between the private life of devotion and the public life of service, an oft-neglected key to Christian living.

Griffin, Emilie. *Clinging: The Experience of Prayer.* San Francisco: Harper and Row, 1984.

Griffin believes we do not know the full depth of prayer until we practice "radical dependence on God"—clinging. This frees us to be genuinely human, worshiping a God who is genuinely divine.

Gritter, George. *When God Was at Calvary.* Grand Rapids: Baker, 1982.

A useful book for Lenten devotional study, Gritter's work considers the last utterances of Jesus from the cross—commonly called the "seven last words of Christ." Despite the book's sermonic flavor, it offers good insight into the eternal significance of Jesus' death on the cross.

Grubb, Norman. *The Liberating Secret.* Fort Washington PA: Christian Literature Crusade, 1978.

Grubb was a son-in-law of the famed African missionary C. T. Studd and a founder of InterVarsity Christian Fellowship. This book cites many experiences from Grubb's own spiritual life to show that God is ready to bless us if we "ask, seek, and knock" for the deeper things of Christian experience.

Guyon, Madame. *Experience the Depths of Jesus Christ.* Fort Washington PA: Christian Literature Crusade, 1984.[7]

Madame Guyon was a seventeenth-century French mystic whose writings powerfully affected the lives of John Wesley, Hudson Taylor, and other Christian leaders. This book is one of her most direct and easily understood works. It has been completely revised to remove archaic terms that would confuse the modern reader. Madame Guyon personifies the best tradition of Christian mysticism—that quest for a daily experience of oneness with the Lord Jesus.

Hallesby, Ole. *Prayer.* Minneapolis: Augsburg, 1975.

This might have been included in the list of devotional classics; its general applicability and the enduring quality of its message certainly deserve the "classic" title. But we have listed it here because it is more inspirational than devotional; in other words, it discusses the dynamics and the results of prayer more than the methods of prayer. Hallesby acknowledges that prayer often is difficult because we do not know what to say to God. But he urges us to speak openly, as with a friend, for that is the essence of the prayer relationship.

Havergal, Frances Ridley. *Kept for the Master's Use.* Grand Rapids: Baker, 1977.[8]

Havergal wrote several inspirational books in addition to her dozens of gospel songs. *Kept for the Master's Use* is her most enduring inspirational book, having been reprinted by various publishers. The book considers a Christian's dedication of self to the Lord's service.

Havner, Vance. *Though I Walk Through the Valley.* Old Tappan NJ: Fleming H. Revell, 1974.

Bereavement is a difficult experience for any of us. Yet we can gain strength by listening to what others say about their ordeal of grief. Vance Havner is a respected Christian author who has written on a wide variety of topics, but here he bares the agony of his soul as he recalls his grief during the long illness and death of his wife. This book can comfort many who are walking the "deep valley" of sorrow.

---

[7]Also available as *Experiencing God Through Prayer* (Springdale PA: Whitaker House, 1984).
[8]Also available in a large print edition from Keatas (New Canaan CT, 1982).

Holmes, Marjorie. *I've Got to Talk to Somebody, God.* Old Tappan NJ: Fleming H. Revell, 1971.[9]

In very forthright, candid terms, the writer records her conversations with God amid the stresses that any modern woman might feel. Often considered the best of Holmes's books, *I've Got to Talk* voices the burden of women's hearts as they are, without pretense. This book is a good model for honest, straight-talking prayer.

Howell, Clinton T. *Harvest of Hope.* Nashville: Thomas Nelson, 1978.

This collection of various inspirational pieces points toward the hope we have in Christ Jesus, regardless of our present circumstances. A good book to pick up and read at odd moments; even random selections are apt to contain something helpful if you are in need of cheer.

Howell, Clinton T. *Joyous Journey.* Nashville: Thomas Nelson, 1978.

A collection of poems, readings, and Scripture passages, Howell's book is designed to revive the discouraged Christian by reminding him that God's great resources are always available.

Hummel, Charles E. *Tyranny of the Urgent.* Downers Grove IL: InterVarsity, 1967.

Hummel challenges our modern tendency to sacrifice the devotional life on an altar of rush schedules and deadlines. In this brief (fifteen-page) essay, he reviews the ministry of Jesus to show that we can cultivate a meaningful life of devotion in the midst of a busy life. He describes the characteristics of a life truly devoted to the Lord. This booklet confronts every serious Christian with the importance of a daily devotional time.

Hybels, Bill. *Christians in the Marketplace.* Wheaton IL: Victor Books, 1982.

An excellent discussion of the stresses that tug at every Christian in the workaday world. None of us can withdraw from the secular (and often ungodly) society around us; in fact, Jesus prayed that we might remain "in the world." Yet a Christian must be distinctively different from the world in which he lives. Hybels considers how this can be so.

John Paul II, Pope. *The Way to Christ.* San Francisco: Harper and Row, 1984.

Compiled from a series of talks that the future pope delivered at Polish student retreats in 1962 and 1972, this book permits us to see the intimately pastoral aspect of his devotional counsel. The talks deal with prayer, spiritual

---

[9]Also available from Doubleday (Garden City NY 1969) and Bantam (New York, 1976).

development, the Eucharist, and a host of other concerns that are important to any Christian, but especially to a Roman Catholic desiring a more disciplined spiritual life.

Johnston, William. *The Way of Christian Mysticism.* San Francisco: Harper and Row, 1984.

A leading Roman Catholic writer reviews the history of Christian mysticism, which he equates with solitary contemplation. He affirms that this mode of spirituality is still crucial to the survival of the Christian community, and he calls other Christians to adopt the self-sacrificing attitude that has char-acterized Christian contemplatives in every age.

Keller, W. Phillip. *Walking with God.* Old Tappan NJ: Fleming H. Revell, 1980.

Keller is best known for his fresh expositions of familiar Bible passages, such as *A Shepherd Looks at the Twenty-Third Psalm?* But here he offers us his reflections on the devotional life. Instead of expounding a given Bible text, he shares out of his own experiences how we can harmonize our lives with the purposes of God. The book deserves to be as widely known as Keller's Bible expositions.

Luther, Martin. *The Table Talk of Martin Luther.* Grand Rapids: Baker, 1979.

Luther first published these talks for laypersons, to encourage them to develop a meaningful spirituality in their daily lives rather than relegating it to the worship services of the church. His fire and enthusiasm still glow from these pages, even though the language is somewhat archaic.

Madden, Myron C. *The Power to Bless.* Nashville: Broadman, 1979.

Christians have largely forgotten their ministry of blessing—the opportunity to pronounce a blessing on a person, object, or situation in God's behalf. Madden believes a careful study of Scripture reveals that this is a vital facet of every Christian's life. An intriguing study that opens new perspectives on the purpose of prayer and personal dialogue.

Marshall, Catherine. *Something More,* large-print edition. Old Tappan NJ: Fleming H. Revell, 1982.[10]

Every earnest Christian longs for a life that is more fully devoted to God—a life that receives more of the blessings of God. Catherine Marshall tells about her own quest for this kind of life and how she found it. A searching set of meditations.

---

[10]Also available from Avon Books (New York, 1976) and Zondervan (Grand Rapids, 1978).

McGinnis, Alan Loy. *The Friendship Factor.* Minneapolis: Augsburg, 1979.[11]

All of us need friends, but some of us seem more adept at making and keeping friends. In this delightful little book, McGinnis uses dozens of real-life illustrations to show how friendship can be built or destroyed. Every growing Christian needs to learn the art of personal relationships that McGinnis so incisively describes.

Miller, Keith. *A Second Touch.* Waco TX: Word, 1982.

A sequel to *The Taste of New Wine,* this book challenges the lethargy and mediocrity that many Christians seem to accept as God's pattern for their lives. Miller describes his own surrender to these twin evils early in his ministry. But he also relates how a fresh enduement of the Holy Spirit enabled him to shake off his spiritual listlessness and move into more ambitious ways of serving Christ. The book summons all Christians to examine their lives and see whether a "second touch" of God's Spirit is not needed.

Miller, Keith. *The Taste of New Wine.* Waco TX: Word, 1982.

A successful executive in the oil exploration business, Miller became disgusted with the hollowness of his life. He answered a call to Christian ministry and went to seminary to begin preparing for the pastorate. But soon he discovered the mainline churches were just as hollow as the ambitious business career he'd left. Then he came in contact with a few groups of Christians who were vibrantly alive and growing in their relationship with Christ. He began to see this is God's desire for all Christians. *The Taste of New Wine* is a prophetic call for all Christians to rediscover the life that flows from vital relationship with the Lord.

Miller, William A. *Make Friends with Your Shadow.* Minneapolis: Augsburg, 1981.

The Bible calls it our "carnal" nature; psychologists call it our "shadow self." Whatever one chooses to call it, every Christian recognizes the existence of a rebellious alter ego within, which seems to emerge at the most embarrassing moments. Hospital chaplain William Miller has observed this "shadow" at work in his patients—and in himself—for many years. Here he suggests how the "shadow self" can be disciplined.

Mueller, George. *Answers to Prayer.* Chicago: Moody, 1984.

Mueller had an astonishing ministry among the orphans of Wales at the turn of the century, depending entirely upon the provisions God would supply in

---

[11]Also available in Spanish as *La Amistad Factor Decisivo* (El Paso TX: Casa Bautista De Publicaciones, 1982).

answer to prayer. This book records some of the unusual answers that God gave to his pleas for help.

Nouwen, Henri J. M. *Out of Solitude*. Notre Dame IN: Ave Maria, 1974.

This simple yet powerful book of meditations considers the importance of cultivating a life of meditation and prayer. Its three chapter titles outline the movement of a life of authentic Christian spirituality: "Out of Solitude," "With Care," "In Expectation." Nouwen is a Dutch Roman Catholic priest who taught for ten years at Yale Divinity School before entering the Abbey of Genesee, New York.

O'Connor, Elizabeth. *Letters to Scattered Pilgrims*. San Francisco: Harper and Row, 1982.

Informally written, these meditations are meant to instill courage and determination in Christians who feel they are stymied in their spiritual growth. O'Connor has a knack for giving us the gospel in common, everyday language rather than the well-worn platitudes so many inspirational writers use. Her confidence in the redemptive power of God and in the resilience of the human spirit can be read in every one of the "letters."

Oldenberg, Cornelius. *Comfort Ye My People*. Grand Rapids: Baker, 1983.

Oldenberg's collection of prayers, poems, and thoughts will speak to the special needs of the grieving. He finds many Scripture passages of comfort and assurance for the bereaved. A suitable gift booklet.

Olford, Stephen. *Going Places with God*. Wheaton IL: Victor Books, 1983.

Noted Presbyterian minister Stephen Olford takes us on an enriching study of how God guides his people, using as case studies the experiences of Moses, Joshua, and Caleb. This faith-affirming book reminds us that God is just as capable of leading his people today as he did in Bible times.

Ortlund, Raymond C. *Be a New Christian All Your Life*. Old Tappan NJ: Fleming H. Revell, 1983.

Popular conference leader and pastor Ray Ortlund has a gift for identifying the needs of modern Christians and bringing sound Bible insights to answer those needs. Here Pastor Ortlund deals with the problem of losing the joy and vitality that are so common for the new convert. How can someone stay vitally rooted in Jesus, even after years of being a Christian? Ortlund answers with the practical and compassionate air of a pastor who has wrestled with this problem in his own life.

Palms, Roger C. *First Things First*. Wheaton IL: Victor Books, 1983.

Our priorities can get so ensnarled that we begin to wonder how to spend our time and energy. Palms shows how to evaluate your present life priorities—especially your spiritual priorities—and begin to make intentional changes for the better. Most important, he shows what things a maturing believer should value.

Parks, Helen Jean. *Holding the Ropes.* Nashville: Broadman, 1983.

A veteran missionary discusses the importance of intercessory prayer for missions. The work of missions must be undergirded by praying Christians who are willing to persist in seeking God's help for specific needs in the field. The author explains how this kind of intercessory prayer can be most effective, and she offers several missionaries' testimonies of how God has answered these intercessory prayers.

Paxson, Ruth. *Life on the Highest Plane,* 3 vols. Grand Rapids: Baker, 1983.

Paxson examines Scripture promises concerning the privileges and obligations of a Christian. A most thorough Bible study, it will lead you into a deeper appreciation of your high calling in Christ. A Scripture index is included.

Peale, Norman Vincent. *The Power of Positive Thinking.* Old Tappan NJ: Fleming H. Revell, 1966.[12]

The first book to come from the pen of this leading American author, *The Power of Positive Thinking* tells how a Christian can be emboldened in the face of any trying circumstance if he simply thinks and acts in faith. Critics have condemned the simplified concepts of psychology that Peale presents here. Yet an open-minded reader will find that the book clearly exalts Jesus Christ and applies the truth of Scripture.

Penn-Lewis, Jessie and Evan Roberts. *War on the Saints.* Fort Washington PA: Christian Literature Crusade, 1964.[13]

Evil spirits are constantly at work, trying to deceive and discourage the people of God. In this perceptive book, Mrs. Penn-Lewis and Mr. Roberts (a leading evangelist in the Welsh Revival) explain how to recognize these destructive spirits and thwart their influence. We seldom consider this aspect of a Christian's devotional life; yet we must understand the influence of evil spirits as well as that of the Holy Spirit.

Peterson, Eugene H. *A Long Obedience in the Same Direction.* Downers Grove IL: InterVarsity, 1980.

---

[12]Also available from Fawcett Book Group (New York, 1978).
[13]Also available from Thomas E. Lowe, Ltd. (New York, 1984).

A study of the Psalms which outlines the difficulties that any person is likely to encounter in serving God. Peterson emphasizes that spiritual growth results from long-term faithfulness to God, despite the difficulties we encounter.

Rassieur, Charles L. *Christian Renewal: Living Beyond Burnout*. Philadelphia: Westminster, 1984.

Volume 5 in the series of "Potentials" booklets edited by Wayne E. Oates, this book addresses a critical problem that drives many Christians to seek a more meaningful devotional life. Rassieur writes from the perspective of a psychiatric counselor; yet he emphasizes the importance of spiritual renewal in a person's quest for psychological wholeness. Though more sophisticated than most books listed here, it should still be considered inspirational because it well describes the characteristics of a growing Christian life.

Roberts, Robert C. *The Strengths of a Christian*. Philadelphia: Westminster, 1984.

Part of the "Spirituality and Christian Life" series edited by Richard H. Bell, this booklet portrays the virtues of a growing Christian. It also warns of the spiritual and emotional problems one can encounter in the process of growing into the fullness of the stature of Christ. Roberts is professor of philosophy and religion at Western Kentucky University.

Rogers, Adrian. *The Secret of Supernatural Living*. Nashville: Thomas Nelson, 1982.

One might call this a modern Christian's version of Brother Lawrence's *Practice of the Presence of God*. Baptist pastor Adrian Rogers explains how he began to see God at work in the everyday situations of his life, which awakened a fuller appreciation of God's love and care for each of us. Rogers leads us to consider how we can yield ourselves more completely to Christ's lordship in the commonplaces of our daily lives.

Ryle, J. C. *Call to Prayer*. Grand Rapids: Baker, 1976.

Ryle considers the importance of consistent, persistent prayer in every Christian's life. He warns of the grave detriment that comes to a Christian who neglects prayer. And he points us to Jesus' own life as a model of the prayer-immersed living that should be our habit and joy.

Sanders, J. Oswald. *Your Best Years*. Chicago: Moody, 1982.

A delightful study of the special joys of Christian living for the aged. Sanders explains how a person can be vital and healthy in spirit at an advanced age, regardless of the condition of the body. A refreshing book for the elderly Christian—and for those who soon will be.

Schaeffer, Ulrich. *Growing into the Blue.* San Francisco: Harper and Row, 1984.

A book richly illustrated with full-color photographs, *Growing into the Blue* affirms the writer's commitment to keep on growing in Christ. Despite hearing the gloomy predictions of economic depression, nuclear holocaust, and a myriad other catastrophes, Schaeffer believes each Christian should pursue the goal of becoming more like Christ.

Schuller, Robert H. *Tough-Minded Faith for Tender-Hearted People.* Nashville: Thomas Nelson, 1983.

How does a Christian strive for the goals that God sets before him? How should he deal with the spiritual and emotional conflicts that crop up along the way? In this very practical book, Dr. Schuller describes the methods you can use to move toward God's calling. A practical and easy-to-understand book.

Schuller, Robert H. *Tough Times Never Last, But Tough People Do!* Nashville: Thomas Nelson, 1982.[14]

At the top of the *New York Times* best-seller list for several weeks, Schuller's book has brought hope and revitalization to many disheartened people. Each section contains a positive, faith-building concept to strengthen those who feel the situations of life are "getting them down." Simply written, yet built on sound spiritual and psychological principles.

Seamands, David A. *Healing for Damaged Emotions.* Wheaton IL: Victor Books, 1981.

We are apt to think of "healing" only in physical terms; but United Methodist pastor David Seamands points out that emotional healing is just as urgently needed. He lifts episodes from his own pastoral counseling to show the devastating effects of unresolved emotional problems. Then he shows how we can move toward healing, the restoration of emotional wholeness, with God's grace.

Seamands, David A. *Putting Away Childish Things.* Wheaton IL: Victor Books, 1982.

In a sequel to *Healing for Damaged Emotions,* Dr. Seamands visualizes a mature Christian personality and examines the immature habits and attitudes we must leave behind as we strive for that maturity. Written in clear and simple style, this book will confront Christians of all ages to go farther in their discipleship.

---

[14]A large-print edition is available from G. K. Hall (Boston, 1984). A condensed version is available on sixty-minute tape cassette from Thomas Nelson (Nashville 1984).

Simpson, A. B. *The Gentle Love of the Holy Spirit.* Camp Hill PA: Christian Publications, 1984.

Formerly titled *Walking in the Spirit,* this book describes the character of a Spirit-filled life and how we can allow the Holy Spirit full access to our entire being. It is full of refreshing truths for Christians who seek a higher spirituality than they have known thus far.

Simpson, A. B. *The Self Life and the Christ Life.* Camp Hill PA: Christian Publications, 1967.

"The love of this world is enmity with God," the Bible says, and Simpson shows the striking contrast between loving the world and loving Christ. Too often we have been beguiled into thinking that Christ values the same things that the world values; but that is manifestly absurd. Modern Christians should ponder these pages with care.

Smith, Hannah Whitall. *The Christian's Secret of a Happy Life.* Old Tappan NJ: Fleming H. Revell, 1968.[15]

In this classic inspirational book, Mrs. Smith deals with the everyday concerns of a Christian—how to trust God to provide for physical needs, how to find relief from anxiety and fear, and how to renew the inner wellsprings of joy. She cites many analogous problems in our dealings with family members, neighbors, merchants, and the like—pointing out that we can apply to our spiritual experience the common-sense solutions we have long applied to our social experience. This book is a very easy one to comprehend and implement.

Speas, Ralph. *How to Deal with How You Feel.* Nashville: Broadman, 1980.

Emotions should be an asset to every Christian, allowing one to express the deepest convictions in a lively and convincing way or to respond with compassion to the needs of another. But mishandled emotions can be a liability as well, interfering with one's communication with God and luring one away from wholehearted service. Speas takes up the most troubling emotions that are common to a Christian—loneliness, guilt, and depression—showing how we can turn these emotions to the service of God.

Taylor, Jack R. *The Key to Triumphant Living.* Nashville: Broadman, 1978.[16]

Taylor had long been pastor of a large Southern Baptist church when he discovered that God's Holy Spirit was bringing renewal to the church. Here he

---

[15]Also available from Zondervan (Grand Rapids, 1984) and in a large-print edition from Fleming H. Revell (Old Tappan NJ, 1983).
[16]Also available in a Spanish edition, *La Llave para una Vida de Triumfo* (El Paso TX: Casa Bautista De Publicaciones, 1982).

describes what happened, and how other churches can open themselves to the reviving work of God's Spirit as well.

Taylor, Jack R. *Prayer: Life's Limitless Reach.* Nashville: Broadman, 1977.
"Nothing lies beyond the reach of prayer," Taylor writes, "because nothing lies beyond the reach of God." This victorious book stakes out the broad horizons of a Christian's prayer life, challenging us to commit ourselves to more ambitious and expectant prayer.

Thompson, Conrad M. *Mender of Broken Hearts.* Minneapolis: Augsburg, 1982.
Thompson has long been the featured speaker on the "Lutheran Vespers" radio program. In colorful and practical terms, he addresses the needs of people who are bereaved, divorced, or battered by other difficulties in life. *Mender of Broken Hearts* reminds us that God is able to heal our soul wounds as well as our physical ones.

Tozer, A. W. *I Talk Back to the Devil.* Camp Hill PA: Christian Publications, 1972.
These twelve sermons refute the objections and excuses often raised when we consider a life of Christian perfection. Tozer explains that every Christian has the privilege of growing more like Christ every day, and God's Holy Spirit provides the ability to overcome Satan's efforts to deter us.

Tozer, A. W. *Man: The Dwelling Place of God.* Camp Hill PA: Christian Publications, 1966.
What is the full spiritual potential of men and women today? Tozer reveals some startling answers in this classic exposition of Bible passages that deal with Christian growth and sanctification. Defeated Christians can take new courage from the Bible promises unfolded here.

Tozer, A. W. *The Pursuit of God.* Camp Hill PA: Christian Publications, 1948.[17]
Tozer pastored churches in St. Paul, Minnesota and Toronto before becoming editor of *The Alliance Weekly* (now *The Alliance Witness*) where he wrote boldly in defense of the Christian faith for many years. He describes the soul's hunger to know more of God and the delights of a relationship with God that grows deeper each day. Tozer shares out of his own experience and his pastoral observations so that we can see such a relationship can be obtained here and now. This little volume, which many feel is Tozer's best inspirational

---

[17]Also available in a large-print edition from Fleming H. Revell (Old Tappan NJ, 1982).

book, ranks beside Brother Lawrence's *The Practice of the Presence of God* and other great classics of devotion.

Watchman Nee. *A Balanced Christian Life.* Fort Washington PA: Christian Literature Crusade, n.d.

A collection of ten sermons on the qualities of a growing Christian, this book is considered by many to be one of the best inspirational books to be written in this century. Watchman Nee clearly speaks from his own experience of spiritual wrestling and pain. A victorious, uplifting book.

Webbe, Gale D. *The Night and Nothing.* San Francisco: Harper and Row, 1983.

How does a Christian handle times of spiritual dryness, loneliness, and seeming estrangement from God? Webbe shows that these dark, deserted places are to be expected on our spiritual pilgrimage. He shares from his own experience how such "dark" times can help us gain a better understanding of who God is and what he is calling us to become. Webbe is an Episcopal priest.

Wells, Albert M., Jr. *As Touching the Holy.* Grand Rapids: Baker, 1980.

Wells quotes a variety of Christian authors on the subject of prayer—why it is needed, what transpires, and how it can be developed. This is a treasury of wisdom from some of the most notable Christian leaders who have ever lived, skillfully chosen and presented to good effect.

Wiersbe, Warren W. *Songs in the Night.* Grand Rapids: Baker, 1981.

Taken from the radio program by the same name that Wiersbe hosted while pastor of Chicago's Moody Memorial Church, this book offers gentle pastoral counsel on matters of everyday Christian living. A comforting book that would be especially good for someone experiencing spiritual or emotional difficulties.

Chapter Four
Daily Devotionals

A few nineteenth-century writers such as Andrew Murray compiled books of daily devotional readings; but the years since World War I witnessed a proliferation of such books and magazines. They are quite popular today. I think this is a symptom of the hectic pace of our time, in which most Christians feel they cannot afford long periods of concentrated devotional reading. A collection of daily readings can handily solve this problem. It serves up morsels of spiritual food each day, not overwhelming the reader with its richness, yet enticing one to read more.

I believe we will see our leading pastors and evangelists publish an even greater array of daily devotionals for the remainder of this century. And I would venture to guess that some of the most enduring devotional books of the twentieth century will be of this type.

No one can deny that the daily devotional book or magazine serves a useful function in the spiritual discipline of a new Christian. As a pastor, I often gave new Christians a copy of a devotional magazine a few days after that person made a decision for Christ. The devotional magazine began to build spiritual soundness into the new Christian's life at a time when temptation and doubting were sure to come. It offered a simple way to begin a daily devotional time with the Lord. Since each reading took just a few minutes, the daily devotional trained a new convert in this habit a small step at a time; yet one could see immediate results: the sense of assurance, the growing commitment to Christ, and the expanding spiritual knowledge of the person who read the daily devotional.

The daily devotional book or magazine is of positive help to a more mature Christian as well. Perhaps one has grown spiritually apathetic with the passing years. Or continued training has made one knowledgeable concerning the Bible, church history, and theology, while the personal relationship with Christ has been neglected. Do these words describe you? Then a spiritual "refresher course" may be needed, and the daily devotional can help you reawaken the ardor of your relationship with the Lord.

Various Approaches

You will discover that daily devotional books and magazines take various approaches to their theme. Here are some of the most common formats:

Sequential Bible Study. Some daily devotionals lead you through a study of a section of the Bible or of a certain biblical theme. *The Daily Walk* magazine takes you through the entire Bible in a year's time, for example. (The editors award you a certificate for completing the year's study.) Other devotional magazines such as *Pathways to God* take you through a cycle of Bible readings that coincide with the Sunday School curriculum readings, the lectionary, or some other multi-year Bible reading plan. Still others guide you through a series of Bible readings related to the phases of the church year (Epiphany, Lent, Pentecost, and so on). By using a daily devotional that follows such a planned sequence of Bible readings, you can gain a more well-rounded knowledge of God's Word.

Random Bible Readings. Some daily devotionals seem to value variety above order; their readings follow no logical sequence, but give you a mixture of Scripture texts and topics every week. Some readers prefer this approach because they feel more likely to chance upon a reading that will speak to their need on a given day. The most popular daily devotional books, such as Oswald Chambers's *My Utmost for His Highest,* have been compiled in this fashion. An overarching theme may be detected, but each day's installment has an element of surprise.

Sequential Theme Study. E. Stanley Jones follows this pattern quite capably in his series of daily devotional books. Each volume addresses a theme—such as the abundant life that Christ offers us—and unfolds that theme in a systematic way which anticipates the reader's questions and objections. One would not expect a daily devotional book to be theologically sophisticated; but Jones proves otherwise. His books are like systematic theologies for the common man. Few other devotional writers have been able to execute a systematic study of Christian teachings so deftly in a daily devotional book.

Extracts from Devotional Classics. To introduce readers to the great devotional literature of the past, some editors have gathered bits from a variety of writers to create new daily devotional books. Mrs. Charles Cowman's book, *Streams in the Desert,* is a beautiful example of this; it includes readings from F. B. Meyer, Andrew Murray, and dozens of other well-known devotional writers. Books of this kind may seem uneven in the style of writing and the richness of thought from one day to the next, depending on the editor's skill. Yet they can broaden our horizons of devotional reading. Occasionally, a single devotional classic is divided into daily readings; for example, Fleming H. Revell issued such an edition of Hannah Whitall Smith's *The Christian's Secret of a Happy Life* in 1984.

Using the Daily Devotional

Select a daily devotional book or magazine that deals with subjects that interest you. It's a mistake to embark on a daily study program simply because a friend has recommended it or because the author is one of your favorites. And perhaps the devotional material now in vogue does not speak to your spiritual needs. Don't be afraid to choose the devotional resources that do speak to you, regardless of what is popular. The preface or introduction of the book should describe the focus of its study; if not, browse through a few selections in the book until you can discern what it has to offer.

Also check the Bible version that is the key reference for the daily devotional. You should have little problem using material that is based on one of the standard versions (KJV, NKJV, RSV, NASB, or NIV); but beware of a devotional based on more loosely translated "dynamic equivalence" versions or paraphrases such as the *Living Bible*. Because these are designed to give a more general sense of each passage, there is greater likelihood that any day's devotional text will fail to convey the full sense of its Scripture context.

Examine the daily devotional to see how much time it requires of you each day. A devotional book that gives you a couple of Scripture verses and a one-page meditation will not demand as much time as one that assigns two or three chapters of Scripture or gives you a series of involved devotional exercises. How much time do you plan to allocate to your devotional period? How much concentration will you be able to give to your devotions, in view of the time of day, your surroundings, and the physical energy you are likely to have? If you answer these questions honestly, you will be better prepared to evaluate how useful a certain devotional book or magazine might be for you.

Consider the results you anticipate. Will this resource provide you opportunity to improve your Bible knowledge? to cultivate a different attitude toward prayer? to become more aware of human needs around you? I believe this is the most crucial test of any devotional resource: how it is likely to affect my outlook as a Christian.

After you have selected an appropriate resource for your daily devotions, review Chapter 1 of this *Resource Guide* for instruction in how to start your daily devotional time. If your devotions are cut short now and then, or if you are unable to have your devotional period for some reason, do not lose heart. Take it as an opportunity to renew your pledge to the Lord. Confess your limitations and weaknesses, claiming his strength to help you keep this devotional commitment each day. Then pick up the devotional study again. If your readings are dated to coincide with special events of the church year, you may need to skip over some material to get "back in step" with the reading plan. But don't let this lapse turn you to despair. Keep on reading, praying, and meeting with the Lord as you promised you would. He will bless your perseverance.

A Devotional Study Group

Perhaps you have thought of joining or starting a Bible study group in your neighborhood. Thousands of these groups have sprung up in the last twenty years. They provide a supportive climate in which Christians can read and apply Scripture to their daily lives. Why not begin a neighborhood devotional group. I think such a group could yield great benefits:

First, a devotional study group would encourage more practical Bible study. Since the chief aim of the group is more authentic Christian worship and spiritual growth, the group is more likely to employ Bible insights in their personal lives. (See the section on devotional Bible study in my book, *Bible Study Resource Guide,* rev. ed., pp. 193–198). Bible study in a devotional group should not be allowed to degenerate into mere theologizing; it should help to shape the spiritual character of the participants.

Second, a devotional group will heighten each person's awareness of the essence of the church. Many Christians tend to view the church as an institution encrusted with precious traditions and entwined with bureaucratic procedure. A neighborhood devotional group helps us realize that the church is essentially a fellowship of Christian believers—supporting one another, counseling one another, and correcting one another in our journeys of faith. This can be a delightful and liberating realization.

Third, a devotional group provides the Lord with an effective channel for his Holy Spirit to influence our lives. The Spirit influences us in our moments of solitude, of course; but the Lord promised that his Spirit would be sensibly present whenever "two or three are gathered together in my name" (Matt. 18:20). He is present each time we worship him; but when we worship with a few trusted Christian friends who are growing with us in a life of intentional devotion to him, the Spirit of Christ takes on human flesh once again. He speaks through their voices, listens through their ears, and comforts through their extended hands.

Why not give the Lord this unique opportunity to minister to you, by ministering to him through a neighborhood devotional group

ANNOTATED BIBLIOGRAPHY

Adeney, Carol, ed. *This Morning with God.* Downers Grove IL: InterVarsity, 1978.

Alternating between series of readings from the Old and New Testaments, this guide takes you through the entire Bible in four years. Questions aid you in probing the Scripture reading each day to glean more insights. A good introduction to inductive Bible study.

Baker, Pat. *A Minute in the Morning.* Grand Rapids: Baker, 1984.

Pat Baker is the mother of three and grandmother of two; so she knows first-hand how difficult it is for a homemaker to observe the discipline of a daily devotional time. But *A Minute in the Morning* provides 150 brief devotional readings that can start a woman on her way to a good devotional time, even if it is hard to find the time.

Barnett, Joe R. *Just for Today.* Grand Rapids: Baker, 1979.

These concise Scripture outlines will take you through the entire Bible in a year. Barnett gives a minimum of inspirational comment so that you can spend most of your devotional time reading Scripture itself.

Bitzer, Heinrich. *Light on the Path.* Grand Rapids: Baker, 1982.

For the serious student of biblical languages, this devotional gives a selection from the Hebrew Old Testament and the Greek New Testament each day. A good tool for keeping your linguistic skills sharp as well as cultivating a better devotional life.

Bjorge, James R. *Forty Ways to Say I Love You.* Minneapolis: Augsburg, 1978.

Especially for newlyweds or those about to be married, this book of forty meditations will help a couple find a variety of ways to communicate their love for one another and their love for God. It's a popular gift book.

Bosch, Henry G. *Rainbows for God's Children in the Storm.* Grand Rapids: Baker, 1984.

Bosch was a long-time contributor to the *Our Daily Bread* devotional magazine published by "Radio Bible Class." This new daily devotional brings together some of his best articles to answer the needs of suffering, stress-filled Christians. It is an uplifting and faith-emboldening response to the troubles that come to all of us at some time.

Bryant, Al. *Today, Lord, I Will.* Waco TX: Word, 1982.

An action-oriented devotional, this book begins each day with a Scripture text, leads you into a time of quiet meditation, then calls you to practice what God has revealed during your devotional time. This clear emphasis on living your spiritual insights is rare in daily devotional books.

Caldwell, Louis O. *Good Morning, Lord: Devotions for College Students.* Grand Rapids: Baker, 1971.

Dr. Caldwell is a respected counselor who has written several books for college students, most notably *After the Tassel Is Moved.* Now he has compiled a brief book of daily devotionals for college students which speaks to some of the common problems that students encounter. A frank and reassuring book.

Carmichael, Amy. *Whispers of His Power.* Old Tappan NJ: Fleming H. Revell, 1983.

Based on the hundreds of letters that Miss Carmichael wrote during her missionary tour in India, this daily devotional conveys the personal warmth one would expect to find in a letter from a Christian friend. Her writings radiate hope and joy, despite the many hardships Miss Carmichael suffered at her post.

Chambers, Oswald. *Daily Thoughts for Disciples.* Grand Rapids: Zondervan, 1984.[1]

Though not as clearly centered on the Bible as Chambers's devotional, *My Utmost for His Highest,* this book is nonetheless helpful in the everyday spiritual struggles of a Christian. This devotional was compiled after his death from Chambers's various writings.

Chambers, Oswald. *My Utmost for His Highest.* New York: Dodd, Mead, and Company, n.d.[2]

Perhaps the best-known daily devotional written in this century, Chambers's book calls us to a life of full surrender to Christ's service. Each day's reading is based upon a Scripture text. A most challenging and soul-stirring book, its power has not diminished with the passing years.

Chambers, Oswald. *Still Higher for His Highest.* New York: Dodd, Mead, & Company, 1963.[3]

This fitting sequel to *My Utmost for His Highest* exhorts maturing Christians to spend much time in deep Bible study and prayer. Chambers believed God is calling for women and men who are willing to devote their minds and bodies to his service, as well as their souls. *Still Higher* implores us to discipline our lives so that we may be more effective servants for Christ.

Cooper, Davis. *Daily Devotions for Newlyweds.* Nashville: Broadman, 1983.

Three months of daily devotional readings are contained in this attractively bound gift book. Readings deal with the attitudes and priorities that make for a healthy Christian marriage. Several have exercises in husband-wife communications to help the newlywed couple develop their skills of relating to one another in the home environment.

---

[1]Also available from Christian Literature Crusade (Washington PA, 1983).
[2]Also available from Thomas Nelson (Nashville, 1983) and in a large-print edition from Fleming H. Revell (Old Tappan NJ, 1983).
[3]Also available from Christian Literature Crusade (Fort Washington PA, 1970) and in a large-print edition from (Grand Rapids, n.d.).

Cowman, Mrs. Charles E. *Streams in the Desert.* Grand Rapids: Zondervan, 1965.

Mrs. Cowman compiled these daily devotionals during her years of missionary service in Japan and China. First published in 1925, this book has gone through many editions and translations so that today it may be found in virtually every country of the world, with over two million copies in print. Each day has a Scripture reading, an excerpt from a great inspirational writer, and a closing thought from Mrs. Cowman.

Daily Light on the Daily Path. Nashville: Thomas Nelson, 1982.

This daily devotional has been a favorite of evangelical Christians for many years. Comprised mainly of Scripture readings, the devotional takes you through every great theme of the Bible in a year's time. This edition uses Scripture texts from the *New King James Version.*

Draper, Edythe, ed. *In Touch.* Wheaton IL: Tyndale House, 1971.

Featuring daily selections from the *Living Bible,* this devotional book has been well received by Christians who like the plainly worded paraphrases of Kenneth Taylor. This book is available in several gift editions for special occasions.

Everett, Betty Steele. *Who Am I, Lord?* Minneapolis: Augsburg, 1983.

Here is a book of story devotions for girls aged eight to twelve, an important life-changing time for every young woman. The stories explore various roles that God may call a girl to fulfill as she enters womanhood. A Bible verse and prayer conclude each day's reading.

Fant, Clyde E., Jr. *The Best of Open Windows.* Nashville: Broadman, 1981.

Selected from the popular Baptist devotional magazine, *Open Windows,* this gift book ranges across a variety of inspirational themes. W. A. Criswell, C. Roy Angell, and other well-known Baptist writers are among the contributors.

Foster, Harry. *Daily Thoughts on Bible Characters.* Fort Washington PA: Christian Literature Crusade, 1978.

A most unusual book of daily devotions, this volume examines a different Bible character for each day of the year. We can learn much about the molding of our own Christian character by considering the experiences of these great (and not-so-great) people of Bible times.

Havergal, Frances Ridley. *Opened Treasures.* Neptune NJ: Loizeaux Brothers, 1962.

Frances Ridley Havergal (1836–79) is well known for her hymns and gospel songs, which are still included in modern hymnals. This fascinating volume takes up a Scripture reading each day with an appropriate comment from Havergal's inspirational writings and a few lines from one of her songs.

Havergal, Frances Ridley. *The Royal Invitation and Loyal Responses.* Grand Rapids: Baker, 1978.

Actually a combination of two books, each with thirty-one meditations, this would be quite appropriate for a two-month devotional study. *The Royal Invitation* ponders thirty-one Bible instances in which the Lord says, "Come!" *Loyal Responses* considers people who answered that call and how the response changed their lives forever.

Havner, Vance. *Day by Day with Vance Havner.* Grand Rapids: Baker, 1984.

Here is another down-to-earth devotional book from the beloved evangelist Vance Havner. Unlike many devotional books which remain on a superficial level of sentimentality, Havner's delves into some controversial problems such as the commercialization of the church and the spiritual lethargy of modern pastors. So this book rings the chime of a prophet as well as the gentle bell that calls us to prayer.

Havner, Vance. *The Vance Havner Devotional Treasury.* Grand Rapids: Baker, 1981.

A daily devotional for a full year, gleaned from the sermons and books of a noted American evangelist. Havner had a gift for plain speech, being able to call out the problems of our day and apply Christ's answers in a most lucid and persuasive way.

Hembree, Ron. *Good Morning, Lord: Devotions for New Christians.* Grand Rapids: Baker, 1983.

New Christians are the first to ask, "How can I start a daily devotional time?" Hembree's book can help them. Each day's reading deals with a problem or temptation that the new Christian is likely to face, drawing on Scripture for guidance to meet these challenges. Another benefit of the book is that it gives the reader a Scripture passage from every book of the Bible, thus introducing him to the sundry riches to be found in God's Word.

Hembree, Ron. *Good Morning, Lord: Devotions for Newlyweds.* Grand Rapids: Baker, 1982.

This book can be used by a newlywed couple to start their daily devotional time together. Its readings touch upon the considerations for building a Christ-centered marriage; but it contains a great deal of inspirational help for an individual Christian's spiritual growth as well. Every Christian couple should cultivate the habit of having a daily devotional time together, and Hambree's book is an excellent resource for beginning it.

Hendricks, William C. *Good Morning, Lord: Devotions for Boys.* Grand Rapids: Baker, 1974.

As a pastor I recommended this book as a gift for several boys entering junior high or middle school. Hendricks's daily readings use illustrations from sports, nature, science, and other fields that interest boys. And he has a way of expressing spiritual truth that does not sound the least "preachy."

Johnson, Lois Walfrid. *Come As You Are.* Minneapolis: Augsburg, 1982.

Young people entering adolescence often feel awkward and self-conscious about their own abilities; they wonder how well they will be accepted by their peers. This book of fifty-five daily devotionals underscores the fact that God invites us into the adventure of adulthood as we are—acne and all—and he is ready to help the teenager find purpose and self-acceptance in these difficult times. For ages twelve to fourteen.

Jones, E. Stanley. *Abundant Living.* Nashville: Abingdon, 1976.

As I mentioned, Jones has given us a rather unique kind of daily devotional that takes the reader step-by-step through the development of a vital Christian truth. In this book, he considers the reader's search for a fulfilling and enjoyable life. He discusses in turn the various ways in which people have tried to obtain such a life, showing that all of these self efforts fail. Then Jones turns to the claims of Jesus Christ, who promised this abundant life to all who wish to have it. A thoughtfully written, yet simple devotional book.

Jones, E. Stanley. *The Way.* Nashville: Abingdon, 1984.

Jones spent several years in India, first as a Methodist missionary, then as a leader of interfaith conferences and retreats. So he saw firsthand the competing claims of various religions that were supposed to be "the true way" for living. Yet the most ardent followers of these religions seemed to be the most restless and belligerent people Jones had ever met. "Men cannot get along with each other because they cannot get along with themselves," Jones observes, "and they cannot get along with themselves because they cannot get along with God" (p. 1). This daily devotional considers God's way for everyday living and how we can be sure we are on his way.

Krutza, William J. *Devotionals for Modern Men.* Grand Rapids: Baker, 1968.

Krutza recognizes the issues that concern most men today—career advancement, personal budgeting, marriage and family relationships, developing a sense of self-esteem, and so on. Such issues emerge often in the course of these daily readings tailored for men. A book without sentimentality or "gee-whiz" religiosity.

Mainprize, Don. *Good Morning, Lord: Meditations for Teachers.* Grand Rapids: Baker, 1974.

An excellent gift book, *Meditations* reminds the reader of the opportunities for Christian service in the classroom and the ideal for which a Christian teacher should strive. A fitting resource for the start of a Christian teacher's day.

Martin, Paul. *Good Morning, Lord: Devotions for Teens.* Grand Rapids: Baker, 1962.

Too many teenagers lose interest in the Christian life and drift away from the church because no one there seems to be talking their language. Martin's daily devotional helps to correct that problem. Taking incidents from the life of a real teenager, he reflects on the sometimes comic and sometimes tragic struggle of being a Christian teen. This is a frank yet fully evangelical book.

Martin, Paul. *More Devotions for Teens.* Grand Rapids: Baker, 1973.

Here Martin moves beyond the private, introspective devotionals of his first book for teens. He considers what a Christian teen can do to resist the moral and spiritual erosion in his peer group. These devotionals call a teen to take a stand against drugs, promiscuity, and the other norms of a secular teenage crowd. It's a call to become one of God's leaders for the future by being courageous for him today.

Mattson, Lloyd. *Good Morning, Lord: Devotions for Men.* Grand Rapids: Baker, 1979.

Rarely does one find a good daily devotional for the working man; but Mattson does an admirable job of meeting this need. His book applies key teachings of Scripture to situations a man is likely to encounter in the office, the factory, or wherever he is called to serve his Lord.

Meyer, F. B. *Devotions and Prayers of F. B. Meyer.* Grand Rapids: Baker, 1979.

Fifty-two devotional readings based on Isaiah comprise this thoughtful book by one of the great inspirational writers of this century. Though not designed strictly as a one-month study, the book is nonetheless useful as a daily devotional resource.

Monsma, Hester. *One Step at a Time.* Grand Rapids: Baker, 1984.

Monsma teaches at a Christian school in western Michigan, so she knows the peculiar challenges of a teacher's day. *One Step at a Time* is a teacher's daily devotional written from inside the educational world. Each reading has a brief Scripture text and a devotional thought related to the classroom.

Mueller, Charles S. *Bible Readings for Teenagers*. Minneapolis: Augsburg, 1982.

A book of one hundred daily Bible readings and meditations for teenagers, this covers a variety of pertinent teen topics—popularity, school, careers, money, and so on. An inexpensive gift book.

Murray, Andrew. *Daily Thoughts on Holiness*. Fort Washington PA: Christian Literature Crusade, 1977.

Andrew Murray earned the respect of Christians around the world through his long years of service in South Africa as a pastor, evangelist, and Bible teacher. This book brings together choice selections from his books *With Christ in the School of Prayer, The Full Blessing of Pentecost, The Spirit of Christ,* and *Waiting on God.* Each selection emphasizes the "deeper life" available to all Christians through the ministry of the Holy Spirit.

Patterson, LeRoy. *Good Morning, Lord: Devotions for Athletes*. Grand Rapids: Baker, 1979.

Drawing on many Scripture passages that allude to athletic contests and the perseverance needed for life, Patterson has compiled a most unique daily devotional for athletes. It challenges the athlete to glorify God with his body as well as his soul, and to see the sports contest as a metaphor of life's spiritual striving to claim the prize of eternal life.

Pearce, J. Winston. *To Brighten Each Day.* Nashville: Broadman, 1983.

The articles in this daily devotional have rather odd titles, perhaps to arouse the reader's interest. But the articles themselves are quite pertinent to the daily problems of Christian living and are solidly scriptural.

Rey, Greta. *Good Morning, Lord: Devotions for Girls.* Grand Rapids: Baker, 1975.

Written primarily for girls of about eight to twelve years of age, this little book deals with peer pressure, family conflict, low self-esteem, and other problems that trouble readers at this time. Sensitively and perceptively written, Rey's book fills an important need.

Reynolds, Lillian Richter. *No Retirement*. Philadelphia: Fortress, 1984.

Mrs. Reynolds is former chairperson of Presbyterian Women (PCUS) and of the Commission on Aging of the Louisiana Interchurch Conference. In this daily devotional, she deals with the unique demands of advancing age, as well as its unique opportunities for growing spiritually.

Rowe, Lois. *On Call: Devotionals for Nurses*. Grand Rapids: Baker, 1984.

The brief Scripture readings and meditations here are designed with a nurse's busy schedule in mind; yet one can survey the entire New Testament and Psalms in a year's time with these readings. The Scripture passages are selected to emphasize healing, interpersonal relations, and other topics of interest to nurses.

Russell, A. J. *God Calling*. Old Tappan NJ: Fleming H. Revell, 1972.[4]

Each day's meditation reminds you of the blessings God has bestowed upon you and the ways in which he is making his will known to you. These selections are also good for reading in public worship services; they create a mood conducive to reverence and worship.

Schlink, Basilea. *More Precious Than Gold*. Carol Stream IL: Creation House, 1978.

This daily devotional is based on the commandments of God, which the Bible says are "more precious than gold." We can find joy in obedience to all things—both the great and small things—God has told us to do.

Shiner, Margaret L. *Good Morning, Lord: Prayers and Promises for Teens*. Grand Rapids: Baker, 1976.

The unusual format of this daily devotional will appeal to teenagers who feel out of touch with God. Each day's reading is a two-way conversation: a Christian teen's prayer to God, followed by God's response of assurance and hope, drawn from the promises of Scripture. It is a faith-building book that should help disheartened teenagers.

Simpson, A. B. *Day of Heaven on Earth*. Camp Hill PA: Christian Publications, 1984.

A reprint of one of Simpson's most cherished inspirational books, this work is just as heart-warming and relevant as it was at the turn of the century. Simpson shows how Christians can begin enjoying the blessedness of Christ's presence and power in their lives now, rather than supposing that those good things must wait for his return.

Sorenson, Stephen. *Growing Up Isn't Easy, Lord*. Minneapolis: Augsburg, 1979.

Boys aged eight to twelve will enjoy these brief story devotions, full of

---

[4]Also available from Jove Publications (New York, 1984).

action and adventure. A short prayer and Bible verse end each day's reading.

Spurgeon, Charles H. *Daily Help.* Grand Rapids: Baker, 1981.[5]

If you like reading Spurgeon's vigorous sermons, filled with real-life illustrations, this book will give you a taste of Spurgeon every day of the year. A half-page meditation each day serves to start your devotional train of thought. All are excerpted from Spurgeon's writings.

Spurgeon, Charles H. *Evening by Evening.* Grand Rapids: Baker, 1975.[6]

This book was created as a companion to Spurgeon's popular daily devotional, *Morning by Morning.* Though it seems to lack the cohesion and discriminating care that made the first volume so strong, this book does have merit, especially if you wish to have Spurgeon continue as your devotional guide.

Spurgeon, Charles H. *Faith's Checkbook.* Chicago: Moody, n.d.

Spurgeon often referred to God's promises as the Christian's "bank account," on which one might draw in time of need. This unique daily devotional offers a Scripture promise for each day of the year, inviting you to claim it as your own.

Spurgeon, Charles H. *Morning by Morning.* Grand Rapids: Baker, 1975.[7]

Spurgeon compiled this daily devotional to aid the spiritual development of the thousands who were converted in his great evangelistic rallies. He emphasized the importance of morning devotions "to anchor the soul so it will not drift away from God during the day."

ten Boom, Corrie. *Each New Day.* Old Tappan NJ: Fleming H. Revell, 1977.

Gathered from Miss ten Boom's many inspirational books and articles, this daily devotional is suffused with the warmth and humor that make her work such a delight to read. If you have read *The Hiding Place,* her account of being imprisoned in a Nazi concentration camp, you know what a resilient faith she had. *Each New Day* gives you a glimpse of the inner genius of Corrie's faith: a humble, trusting self-surrender to the Lord each day.

Todd, Floyd and Pauline Todd. *Good Morning, Lord: Devotions for Campers.* Grand Rapids: Baker, 1973.

Family camping has become a favorite summer pastime for many of us; it provides a rare opportunity for uninterrupted communion with God and with

---

[5]Also available from Putnam Publishing Group (New York, 1959).
[6]Also available from Whitaker House (Springdale PA, 1984).
[7]Also available from Whitaker House (Springdale PA, 1984).

other members of the family. The Todds have written some very appropriate daily devotionals for the camping experience, referring to scenes of nature to remind us of God's presence and his abundant provision for our lives. A good book to read around the campfire for family devotions.

Tozer, A. W. *Renewed Day by Day.* Camp Hill PA: Christian Publications, 1980.[8]

These selections from the writings of Tozer ring with prophetic zeal. One could not call this a comforting or reassuring daily devotional; more often it is disturbing, convicting, and exhorting us to more mature Christian faith.

Turnbull, Ralph G. *At the Lord's Table.* Grand Rapids: Baker, 1967.

These twenty-one meditations on the Lord's Supper are beneficial at any time of year, but especially during Lent. Turnbull invites us to imagine ourselves in the Upper Room, seated at the Lord's Table, sharing that first night of high communion with our Lord.

Vandermey, Mary A. *Love Is Like the Sunlight: Inspirational Thoughts for Teachers.* Grand Rapids: Baker, 1985.

Vandermey is a veteran public schoolteacher who peppers this devotional with humorous and touching incidents from the classroom. The book is divided into sections that correspond to the seasons of the school year, with a separate portion for the "Final Weeks."

Wesley, John. *The Devotions and Prayers of John Wesley.* Grand Rapids: Baker, 1977.

A brief volume of devotional thoughts from one of the great evangelists of the eighteenth century. Each meditation ends with one of Wesley's own prayers. The book is of interest to students of history, but has real inspirational value in its own right.

Daily Devotional Magazines

You may find it easier to establish a daily devotional time with the aid of a devotional magazine. These publications provide brief Scripture readings and devotional readings to help orient your thinking. Many denominations and evangelistic ministries publish daily devotional magazines that are not listed here. Ask Christian friends whether they are acquainted with other such magazines.

Daily Blessing, Oral Roberts Evangelistic Association, 1720 S. Boulder, Tulsa OK 74102.

---

[8]Also available from Gerald B. Smith, ed. (Old Tappan NJ: Fleming H. Revell, 1981).

Contains positive thoughts by evangelist Oral Roberts and members of his ministry staff.

Daily Meditation, Box 2710, San Antonio TX 78299.
Features a daily Scripture reading and a brief comment. Compiled by an independent mission agency.

The Daily Walk, Walk Thru the Bible, P. O. Box 80587, Atlanta GA 30366.
I believe this is one of the best Bible survey devotional magazines now being published. Its plan takes you through the entire Bible in one year. Perhaps more reading than you are accustomed to doing, but a valuable discipline nonetheless. Fascinating Bible facts and anecdotes are presented in a colorful way. The eye-catching design makes the magazine a pleasure to read. And the editors furnish helpful devices for memorizing book outlines and key Bible facts. I recommend this daily devotional magazine for all serious Bible students.

Devotion, Standard Publishing, 8121 Hamilton Avenue, Cincinnati OH 45231.
A nondenominational publication oriented to adults. Easy to read.

Discover the Bible, Archdiocese of Montreal, Bible Center, 2065 Sherbrooke, W., Montreal Que. H3H1G6 Canada.
A devotional guide for studying and praying the biblical readings of each Sunday's Mass. Roman Catholic.

El Hogar Cristiano, Casa Bautista de Publicaciones, Box 4255, El Paso TX 79914.
Contains popular features on Christian home and daily devotions based on the Baptist Sunday School curriculum. Southern Baptist.

Encounter! Baptist Sunday School Board, 127 9th Ave. N., Nashville TN 37234.
Youth daily devotion. Has won several awards for its eye-catching design and the contemporary style of its articles. Southern Baptist.

Good News, Sunday Publications, Inc., 3003 S. Congress Ave., Lake Worth FL 33461.
A homily with scriptural comments for fifty-two Sundays, all holy days, and special occasions. Roman Catholic.

Light Today, 144 Tices Lane, East Brunswick NJ 08816.
Bible reading magazine aimed at younger adults. Colorful, contemporary design. Issued bi-monthly.

My Daily Visitor, Our Sunday Visitor, Inc., Noll Plaza, Huntington IN 46750.
A Roman Catholic devotional magazine published by the staff of *Our Daily Visitor.* Focuses on everyday concerns.

Open Windows, Baptist Sunday School Board, 127 9th Ave. N., Nashville TN 37234.
Daily devotional guide for adults. Large-print edition available. Southern Baptist.

Our Daily Bread, Radio Bible Class, P. O. Box 22, Grand Rapids MI 49555.
One of the best-known daily devotional magazines. Features a daily Scripture reading and a brief meditation, with occasional suggested prayers.

Pathways to God, Warner Press, P. O. Box 2499, Anderson IN 46011.
Each day's article is based on the Scripture reading for the International Sunday School Lesson. Published by the Church of God, but nondenominational in its scope.

Portals of Prayer, Concordia Publishing House, 3558 S. Jefferson, St. Louis MO 63118.
Contains daily Scripture readings, devotional thoughts, and suggested prayers. Published by the Lutheran Church.

Power for Today, Twentieth Century Christian, 2809 Granny White Pike, Nashville TN 37204.
Contains Scripture reading, Bible thoughts, family devotions, hymns, inspirational discussions, and prayer thoughts.

The Upper Room, 1908 Grand Ave., Nashville TN 37202.
A daily devotional guide containing a suggested Scripture reading, a meditation, and a prayer for each day. This has the widest circulation of any daily devotional magazine. Published by an organization related to the United Methodist Church, yet its appeal is nondenominational.

Chapter Five
Inspirational Poetry

Christian poets have touched a responsive chord in the reading public, appealing to people who are bored by other types of Christian books. Yet the unique contribution of inspirational poetry is seldom recognized by libraries, bookstores, or other channels for inspirational literature. Search your local Christian bookstore for books of inspirational poetry; you may find a few "gift books," those collections of effervescent verse with pastel illustrations. But seldom will you find the work of master poets such as T. S. Eliot, W. H. Auden, and Alfred Lord Tennyson. Yet I believe they have as much to say in an inspirational vein as do the "gift book" writers. Must we assume that the "gift book" verse exemplifies the best of Christian poetry?

Each Sunday we sing the soaring hymns of the Christian faith; we often remark that the lyrics opened new insights into our relationship with God. Have we forgotten that hymn lyrics are poetry and that every provocative hymn is really a provocative poem?

Granted, the majority of Christian readers feel perplexed by the obscure symbolism and cryptic vocabulary of modern poets. They would agree with C. S. Lewis in saying, "I am so coarse, the things the poets see/Are obstinately invisible to me."[1] Yet even poetry of the modern free verse style can bring new insights and awaken new appreciation for the ways of God.

Christianity Today, *Christian Century*, *Eternity*, and other leading Christian magazines now publish seasonal Christian verse, often the more introspective and symbolic type which illustrates the deepest convictions of Christianity. Perhaps these publications will encourage the work of Christian poets once again. In an age more oriented to the aural sense than to the reasoning mind, poetry could become a powerful tool for propagating the Christian faith and bolstering the convictions of the faithful.

Let us consider the history of Christian poetry and appraise the unique contribution that poetry can make to the devotional life of Christians today.

---

[1]C. S. Lewis, "A Confession," in *C. S. Lewis: Poems*, ed. by Walter Hooper (New York: Harcourt, Brace and World, 1964), p. 1.

A Brief History of Christian Poetry

The first Christian poems are found in the New Testament. The Book of Revelation weaves a rich tapestry of praise hymns, glorifying the Lamb of God who is crucified, risen, and victorious over Satan and all his minions (Rev. 4:8, 11; 5:9-14; 7:12; 11:17-18; 15:3-4; 16:4-6). Several of Paul's most eloquent statements about the person and ministry of Christ seem to be couched in poetry, and some of these passages may have been sung as hymns by the early Christians (1 Cor. 15:50-54; Eph. 3:14-21; Phil. 2:5-11; 2 Tim. 2:11-13). The Bible records that the earliest Christians sang hymns as part of their worship services (Eph. 5:19; Col. 3:16), and we can be sure these hymns were rich with the symbolism of Christ.

Hymns and poems are scattered throughout the Christian letters that have survived from the ante-Nicene era. Frequently, the governing bishop would suggest a hymn lyric to be sung at baptismal services or other high days on the church's worship calendar. Other hymns were composed by anonymous musicians to celebrate a special event in the life of a congregation. A few of these hymns continued to be sung generation after generation and have trickled into our modern Christian hymnody. Two examples are the *Gloria Patri* and *Te Deum*.

As Christianity spread throughout the Roman Empire, more hymns were circulated in written form so that the scattered congregations could share one another's musical talents. More of these hymns have survived, including "Come, Ye Faithful, Raise the Strain," by John of Damascus (eighth century), and "Christ Is Made the Sure Foundation," by an anonymous writer (seventh century).[2]

Hymns and poems inspired the faith of Christians during the medieval era as well. Bernard of Clairvaux (twelfth century) gave us "Jesus, the Very Thought of Thee," "O Sacred Head Now Wounded," and others. Several hymns have been derived from the prayers of Saint Francis (thirteenth century). And we have a wealth of medieval Advent carols, such as "Good Christian Men, Rejoice" and "Good King Wenceslas." It was during the medieval era that poetry was applied to other tasks of the church, such as recounting its history and translating its Scripture. Bede the Venerable (d. 735) wrote a fascinating history of the English church that preserved much early British poetry and translated some of the Psalms into singable English verse.

Christian liturgy during the Middle Ages reached "a pitch of perfection which was destined not to be surpassed, or indeed maintained."[3] An elaborate

---

[2]See also Eberhard Arnold, ed. *The Early Christians* (Grand Rapids: Baker, 1979), p. 217ff.
[3]Knowles, David and Dimitri Obolensky, *The Middle Ages* (New York: McGraw-Hill, 1968), p. 152.

blending of prayers, songs, and choral responses made the Mass an experience of majestic awe. This flowering of the liturgical arts produced hymns and anthems that are still sung by Protestants as well as Roman Catholics. "O Come, O Come Emmanuel" (twelfth century) is perhaps the most familiar of these. The following stanzas from a lesser known Latin hymn from the fifteenth century suggest the depth of theological reflection and the richness of expression achieved in the hymnody of this period:

> O love how deep, how broad, how high!
>   Beyond man's gift to prophesy—
> That God, the Son of God should take
>   Our mortal form for mortal's sake.
>
> For us baptized, for us He bore
>   His desert fast, and hungered sore;
> For us temptations sharp He knew,
>   For us the tempter overthrew.
>
> For us He prayed, for us He taught,
>   For us His daily works He wrought—
> By words and signs and actions, thus
>   Still seeking not Himself, but us.[4]

The Renaissance, the Reformation, and the Counter-Reformation gave us new treasures of inspirational poetry—not as theologically sophisticated as that of the Middle Ages, yet warmly emotive and provocative. Who could forget the soaring strains of "All People That on Earth Do Dwell" by Thomas Kethe or "Now Thank We All Our God" by Martin Rinkart? This also was a time of great epic poets such as John Milton, whose *Paradise Lost* is still required reading for students of English literature. Milton's unshakable faith in the providence of God is a recurring theme of his poems, as in this brief reflection "On His Blindness":

> When I consider how my light is spent
>   Ere half my days, in this dark world and wide,
>   And that one talent which is death to hide
> Lodged with me useless, though my soul more bent
> To serve therewith my Maker, and present
>   My true account, lest he returning chide—
>   "Doth God exact day-labor, light denied?"

---

[4]"O Love How Deep, How Broad, How High," translated by Benjamin Webb, as published by John W. Peterson and Norman Johnson, eds. *Praise! Our Songs and Hymns* (Grand Rapids: Zondervan, 1979), No. 206.

> I fondly ask; but Patience, to prevent
> That murmur, soon replies: "God doth not need
> Either man's work, or his own gifts; who best
> Bear his mild yoke, they serve him best; his state
> Is kingly: thousands at his bidding speed,
> And post o'er land and ocean without rest;
> They also serve who only stand and wait."

Over the next two centuries, several noted British literary poets also wrote short devotional verse. Among them were William Cowper, Alfred Lord Tennyson, and William Makepeace Thackeray. In America poets such as Henry Wadsworth Longfellow, John Greenleaf Whittier, and Edwin Markham gained respect for their literary accomplishments and left us a rich heritage of Christian verse as well; some of their poems have become hymns of the church.

The twentieth century has produced its share of Christian poets, both serious and lighthearted in their approach. We have already mentioned the names of W. H. Auden, T. S. Eliot, and C. S. Lewis. We might add Edwin A. Robinson, Robert Frost, and Carl Sandburg to that list; though some would question the depth of their Christian convictions, these poets clearly dealt with the deepest matters of faith and life. Well-known theological writers such as Henry vanDyke, Georgia Harkness, and John R. Mott have also expressed themselves in inspirational verse. And we must not overlook the narrative poems and allegories of modern evangelical writers such as Calvin Miller and Thomas Howard. Few of these poets have books of their verse currently in print, but their poems often appear in Christian periodicals and anthologies.

Helen Steiner Rice has distinguished herself as poetess laureate among the writers of popular "gift book" verse. She uses very colloquial terms that convey her thoughts with an ease and immediacy that more sophisticated poets would envy.

The Devotional Reading of Poetry

So we have a great heritage of inspirational verse, written in every era of Christianity. How might we draw on this resource for our devotional times of worship?

First, we may read inspirational verse for its perspective upon the devotional life. The poets who crafted these lines must have grappled with the same problems and triumphs that we experience. A careful reading of their work reveals how they came to understand what was happening in their quiet times with the Lord. Here is a a telling comment from C. S. Lewis for example:

> Master, they say that when I seem
>   To be in speech with you,
> Since you make no replies, it's all a dream
>   —One talker aping two.
>
> They are half right, but not as they
>   Imagine; rather, I
> Seek in myself the things I meant to say,
>   And lo! the wells are dry.[5]

A second way in which inspirational verse can aid our devotional life is by creating an appropriate mood for worship. Some of these poems describe the person and activity of God in such vivid, evocative terms that we begin to sense his presence with us as we read. I have that experience when I read Charles Wesley's hymns or the religious verse of T. S. Eliot; the poet's own sense of God's presence evokes a like sensitivity within me. God indeed is present each time I pause to worship him, but I may not realize his presence unless someone points out the clues. Poets can do this when other writers fail.

Third, inspirational verse heightens our powers of observation, so that we become more aware of our own condition and that of the people around us. Poetry is a very sensual medium; it communicates its message through our senses. So as the poet describes the slow dripping of dew from the forest's canopy overhead, the sweet perfume of a ruby-red rose, or some other observation, we begin to sense the world as the poet does. We begin to notice the emotions that rise within us. We begin to heed the signals of fatigue, contentment, or exhilaration that our bodies give us. And we begin to "read" the expressions of the people with whom we converse each day. We experience the world—and ourselves—with heightened awareness because the poet has sharpened our powers of observation.

You might wish to try writing some inspirational poetry of your own. Try expressing your experiences of the day in verse form. You don't need to struggle for perfect rhyme or meter; but try to choose words that are the most fully descriptive, words that only a keenly observant person could conceive. I believe you will find that God is ready to communicate some profound, life-changing messages in the experiences you have each day, if you are awake to the significance of what is happening. Writing poetry can sharpen your powers of observation, just as reading poetry can. In these ways and more, poetry can introduce you to a more meaningful life of devotion.

---

[5]C. S. Lewis, "Prayer," in *C. S. Lewis: Poems*, edited by Walter Hooper (New York: Harcourt, Brace and World, 1964), p. 122.

ANNOTATED BIBLIOGRAPHY

Bickel, Margot. *Harvest the Day*, ed. by Gerhard E. Frost. Minneapolis: Winston Press, 1984.

This German poet has given us a delightful little book celebrating the g'.c of life. Full-color photographs illustrate these joyous prose poems, whi' .ι point to many pleasant things we can experience each day, if we are aware of them. Swaying trees, rippling streams, and heaving green oceans of grass are some of the exhilarating sights and sounds that God has provided for us; and Bickel's poems bring them to mind.

Black, Patsie. *Tapestry: A Finespun Grace and Mercy*. Portland: Multnomah, 1982.

Vivid images record Miss Black's spiritual pilgrimage and her meditations on the impact Jesus has had upon the course of her life. The terse yet graphic lines let us sense the changing moods of her life and her progressively firmer assurance of her salvation.

deMello, Anthony. *Wellsprings: A Book of Spiritual Exercises*. Garden City NY: Doubleday, 1984.

The author encourages us to use this book of free-verse meditations to prompt our own meditations. In fact, he recommends reading a selection, then putting the book aside to ruminate on its ideas—perhaps even to act them out in mime. The author is a Jesuit priest who directs a retreat center in his native country, India. Many of his poems reflect the traditional Hindu fascination with the spiritual significance of nature.

Dupree, Judith Deem. *Going Home*. Palm Springs CA: Ronald N. Hayes, 1984.

Addressed to a dying friend, these sensitive prose poems do not dwell on reminiscence as do so many books about dying. Rather they focus on the future, on the unimaginable joy that one will know in the presence of Jesus. The poems also ponder the writer's anticipation of being bereaved; they strive to accept the fact of parting and to share the dying friend's eagerness to "go home" to the Lord. Black-and-white photographs illustrate the book.

Eitel, Lorraine, ed. *The Treasure of Christian Poetry.* Old Tappan NJ: Fleming H. Revell, 1982.

This anthology contains over three hundred selections by the foremost Christian poets of all time. It is an excellent resource for pastors and teachers, as well as for personal reading in your devotional time.

Lawson, James Gilchrist, ed. *The Best-Loved Religious Poems*. Old Tappan NJ: Fleming H. Revell, 1981.

Compiled at the turn of the century, this anthology of Christian poems continues to be the favorite of many readers. Lawson arranges the selections by topic, which makes the book quite useful as a resource for sermon preparation.

Leax, John. *The Task of Adam*. Grand Rapids: Zondervan, 1985.

These pensive poems consider the purpose of our everyday "drudge" chores, seeking ways to consecrate even those common activities to the glory of God. John Leax is head of the writing department at Houghton College. His work evidences an appreciation for the literary arts as well a firm commitment to Christ.

MacDonald, George. *Diary of an Old Soul*. Minneapolis: Augsburg, 1965.

MacDonald was a noted British writer of short stories and novels with Christian themes. But here he sets his hand to poetry, giving us a moving inspirational verse for each day of the year.

Pierson, Maurene Fell. *Measuring My Days*. Grand Rapids: Baker, 1978.

Pierson began writing this poetic chronicle of her life when she was diagnosed as having terminal cancer, continuing till her death three years later. The poems well express the peaks and valleys of a Christian's inner turmoil at such a time; yet the confidence of victory shines through even the most gloomy selections. A thought-provoking volume for anyone, but especially for those who are seriously ill.

Rice, Helen Steiner. *Prayerfully*. Old Tappan NJ: Fleming H. Revell, 1971.

Prayers in verse comprise this beautiful little "gift book." One detects in these lines Mrs. Rice's own deep faith in God, tested yet confident and strong.

Rice, Helen Steiner. *Someone Cares*. Old Tappan NJ: Fleming H. Revell, 1972.

This may be the most popular poetry book by Mrs. Rice, who has been called "America's inspirational poet laureate." In traditional rhyme and meter, Mrs. Rice conveys the surety of our faith in God and the inevitable fulfillment of everything he has promised.

Schaffer, Ulrich. *Growing into the Blue*. San Francisco: Harper and Row, 1984.

A book richly illustrated with full-color photographs, *Growing into the Blue* affirms the writer's commitment to keep on growing in Christ. Despite hearing the gloomy predictions of economic depression, nuclear holocaust, and a myriad other catastrophes, Schaffer believes each Christian should pursue the goal of becoming more like Christ.

Shaw, Luci. *Listen to the Green*. Wheaton IL: Harold Shaw, 1971.

Shaw muses about the wonders of nature in this book of tender prose poems. She sees God's providence in the way he has ordered our world, and she teaches us to see that world through new eyes.

Shaw, Luci. *The Sighting*. Wheaton IL: Harold Shaw, 1981.

The "sightings" of these prose poems are the unexpected insights that Mrs. Shaw has encountered. Shaw writes with a keenly observant eye, discerning God's hand in the most ordinary happenings. Yet she does not moralize or sentimentalize about what she sees.

Chapter Six
Christian Fiction and Allegories

A few strait-laced Christians shun novels because they think these books are not "serious reading." Yet some of the most powerful evangelistic tools and the most cogent presentations of life's truth are Christian novels, short stories, and allegories. An imaginative Christian author, with his or her quiver full of bright symbols and true-to-life characters, can strike the target of a reader's mind far more effectively than most theologians or philosophers can. Especially in our day, when the secular world conveys its most important messages through story-like commercials and action-packed films, Christian thinkers are learning again how to be artful storytellers.

I say "learning again" because that is how the earliest Christian teachers communicated the gospel—through stories. In fact, that is how Jesus communicated it.

Jesus' parables were stories that danced and whirled with imaginative genius, even though they were bearing a tray full of truth. A young man estranged from his father, a shepherd seeking a lost lamb, a landowner dividing his assets among three servants—these were the everyday situations that Jesus bent to his purpose of telling the truth in a disarming and memorable way. He used these story lessons to confront the hostile Pharisees. He used them to reassure the puzzled disciples about his death. He used them to foretell the calamitous events that would herald his Second Coming. In each case, his audience was so charmed by the story that they easily remembered it; and that allowed them much later to reflect on the deeper significance of what he had said.

Other Christian teachers have used stories to instruct their people. John Bunyan described the circuitous and danger-fraught spiritual journey of a typical Christian in his allegory entitled *The Pilgrim's Progress*. William Law, in *A Serious Call to a Devout and Holy Life*, used fictitious characters with Latin names to portray the vices of men and women everywhere. In more recent times, Hannah Hurnard has made a peasant girl the subject of her classic story of the Christian life, *Hind's Feet on High Places*. C. S. Lewis has delved into the world of fantasy, creating a queer menagerie of characters to describe our quest for eternal life. And Flannery O'Connor has drawn upon characters from the real world of the rural South—often brutish and unpredictable characters—to show that we must come to grips with evil and suffering if we wish to absorb the whole picture of God's world.

These are just a few of the authors who have employed the craft of fiction in the study of Christian themes. I have mentioned only those who had an overtly Christian purpose in their work; yet we must recognize that other authors such as Charles Dickens, Anthony Trollope, William Faulkner, and Ernest Hemingway have dealt with Christian issues in their fiction as well, even though that was not their avowed purpose. One might make a fascinating study of the Christian symbols in William Shakespeare (as indeed Jean-Jacques Frontain of Purdue University is doing). Another intriguing study is the evolving tone of Roman Catholic fiction, as Catholic novelists try to express the changing role of the church and clerical authority in the lives of the laity (as Richard Gilman and others have done[1]). I mention these to suggest how many writers of fiction are fascinated by the teachings of Jesus and the practical problems of Christian living; even writers who do not profess to be Christians come back to these themes again and again. Of course, a thorough survey of the Christian influence upon world literature is beyond the scope of our concern here.

The Devotional Value of Fiction

Modern novelists have disavowed any desire to communicate a moral or philosophical message through their writings. In their press interviews, writers' conferences, and personal notes they usually assert that they are writing to reflect life as it is—rather than life as it should be. Most are apt to agree with the author who advised aspiring young novelists, "If you have a message to send, try Western Union."

Yet no serious reader of fiction can ignore the fact that every story does have a message, intended or not. Every story reflects the writer's understanding of the purpose (or purposelessness) of human life. We absorb this message as we read. It influences our own understanding of life; it allows us to live fantasies that test some of our aspirations; and it can lead us to modify or reject some of the values we have held for many years.

However, we should not expect a Christian novelist to write with blind optimism, coating every dark corner of life with a veil of simple-minded preachments. A Christian author should come to grips with the hard realities of life, confess perplexity at the mysteries of life, and demonstrate that people of faith may continue to serve their Lord despite their painful, unanswered questions. Francis A. Schaeffer describes the view of life which is common to serious Christian fiction:

---

[1]Gilman, Richard, "Salvation, Damnation and the Religious Novel," *New York Times Book Review* (December 2, 1984), p. 7 ff.

...Christianity is not romantic; it is realistic.

Christianity is realistic because it says that if there is not truth, there is not hope;...In the realm of morals, Christianity does not look over this tired and burdened world and say that it is slightly flawed, a little chipped, and easily mended. Christianity is realistic and says the world is marked with evil and man is truly guilty all along the line. Christianity refuses to say that you can be hopeful for the future if you are basing your hope on evidence of change for the better in mankind. The Christian agrees with the man in real despair, that the world must be looked at realistically, whether in the area of Being or in morals.[2]

Obviously, a novelist with this view will surprise, offend, and occasionally disappoint us in describing the desperate condition of humanity. But by confronting us with the grim truth of human nature, such a novelist can expose the inadequate and superficial moral values we may hold, not to mention our inadequate notions of God. On the other hand, some of us will come away from reading the same author's work filled with our own sense of despair.

For these reasons, we should read fiction critically, not merely for the sake of entertainment. We should be asking analytical questions, such as, "What is this author's understanding of God? of humanity? of suffering? of pleasure? of the greatest good in life?" Careful observation will reveal the moral or spiritual message that a short story or novel is communicating to us; and that revelation gives us the freedom to decide whether we will adopt the message.

This sort of analytical reading will require discipline—perhaps more than you are able to invest in your private devotional time. If so, you might join a Christian reading group to sharpen your analytical skills. Some friends of mine meet once a month to discuss a novel they have chosen to read together. Their discussions range across authors as diverse as Dostoevsky, O'Connor, and Hemingway. But their basic plan remains the same: Each month a different member of the group selects a novel for all to read; it must be one that deals with the issues of life in a way that challenges them to re-examine their own Christian convictions. You might consider joining (or starting) a similar reading group in your neighborhood, using as your first resource one of the books from the annotated bibliography at the end of this chapter.

A Special Genre: The Biblical Novel

Lloyd C. Douglas created a sensation with his novel, *The Robe*, published in 1942. Douglas attempted to describe the world of New Testament times, focusing on the character of a Roman gladiator who was won to Jesus Christ through the testimony of people who had known Jesus personally. The setting,

---

[2]Francis A. Schaeffer, *The God Who Is There* (Downers Grove IL: InterVarsity, 1968), p. 46.

the customs, and the dialogue that Douglas employed in *The Robe* authentically represented life in Bible times; Douglas had spent many hours of careful research to guarantee that. The book was a triumph of imaginative story telling which captured the imagination of thousands, Christian and non-Christian alike. Hollywood film producers made a successful motion picture based on this novel, allowing thousands of viewers to see the attractive power of the gospel presented on the screen.

Douglas's novel was an early example of a powerful new genre of fiction, the biblical novel—that is to say, a novel based on actual events from the Bible. Dozens of novelists have tried their hand at biblical novels in the past four decades. Taylor Caldwell, expressed the motivation behind this type of writing in the preface to *Great Lion of God*: "If I can influence, in this book, only ten people who will follow the advice of Our Lord to 'study the Scriptures,' both the Old and the New Testaments, I will feel I have succeeded."[3]

The biblical novelist hopes to intrigue readers with a story that will encourage them to study the Bible itself. The story may assume epic proportions, as with the novels of Douglas and Caldwell, or it may unfold on a less ambitious canvas, as with the novels of Lois Henderson and Joyce Landorf. Yet regardless of its scope, the purpose of the biblical novel is to pique the curiosity of readers toward a deeper investigation of Scripture itself.

Allegories and Fantasies

Here are two other important categories of Christian fiction. The allegory is a fanciful story that portrays moral or spiritual truths by following the adventures of characters who are clearly symbolic, as in John Bunyan's *Pilgrim's Progress*, written in the seventeenth century. Bunyan's story revolves around the pilgrimage of a young man named Christian (obviously representing a new convert to Jesus Christ), who is traveling to a beautiful walled city known as the Celestial City (representing heaven). Along the way, Christian encounters a variety of characters who attempt to dissuade him from his destination. These trying, sometimes comical experiences typify what a new Christian encounters on the way to his eternal home.

The fantasy is a much more fanciful story, often set in an imaginary land with rather bizarre characters who have unusual names and must deal with supernatural (even magical) forces that surround them. All of us are acquainted with the childhood fairy tales which tell of dragons, witches, sorcerers, and enchanted kingdoms. Christian fantasies, such as C. S. Lewis's *Chronicles of Narnia*, are likewise peopled with whimsical characters who have extraordi-

---

[3]Taylor Caldwell, *Great Lion of God* (Greenwich CT: Faucett Publications, 1970), pp. 8-9.

nary experiences. They symbolically illustrate spiritual experiences, as do the Christian allegories; but because of their more dreamlike nature, the fantasies may hold our imagination over the course of a long narrative more effectively than the allegories.

Another advantage of the fantasies is their ability to fascinate children. A good example is George MacDonald's *Back of the North Wind*, which describes how a girl with a terminal illness was taught to face the reality of suffering and death through her nighttime conversations with the wind. This story communicates the sober facts about suffering and death, along with the Christian message of hope for eternal life, to adults and youngsters alike.

Youth Fiction

We should note that thousands of Christian readers have been given a taste for fiction through reading series of young people's novels, such as those by Grace Livingston Hill and the Danny Orlis stories by Bea Palmer. These books are usually focused on a teenage character with whom teenage readers can readily identify; they deal with life issues that are typical for teenagers, such as peer pressure; and they are told in rather simple vocabulary so that young people with limited reading skills can still enjoy them. Several generations of teenage readers have enjoyed these "formula novels" for young people. These books have whetted their appetite for the continued reading of Christian fiction after they enter adulthood.

One word of caution if you plan to buy a Christian youth novel for a young friend or relative: Some of the classic youth novel series, such as the Grace Livingston Hill books, are now quite dated; their old-fashioned setting and dialogue show that they were written many years ago. Some of these series are being revised and updated; but be careful to check the book you plan to buy. Do not choose the old-fashioned version. It may have thrilled the bobby-sox generation thirty years ago, but it will leave modern youth cold.

Inspirational Romances

A new type of Christian novel, which has appeared on the scene since the 1970s, is the inspirational romance. Imitating the style (and often the plot) of secular romance novels, these books attempt to deal with spiritual themes in the context of a romance story. Yvonne Lehman, an experienced writer of inspirational romances, tells what the reader of an inspirational romance can expect from reading such a book:

> . . . A good, captivating story has unfolded and come to a conclusion. Two people have found a kind of love they want to share with each other for the rest of their

lives, through marriage. Someone in the story has been influenced by another's basic moral values and Christian faith, and both the hero and heroine express this belief.

The purpose of an inspirational romance writer should be to give readers not only a few hours of pleasurable escape and entertainment, but a Christian concept to carry with them and help make their lives more meaningful, more loving, and their love lives more inspiring![4]

Janette Oke was one of the first writers of the inspirational romance; her series of novels set in the Old West highlight the most important Christian values, yet deal with struggles that are typical of a woman's everyday life, both then and now.

Various Christian publishers have begun issuing series of mass-market paperback romances. Most of these have contemporary settings and conflict situations. Unfortunately, the short life of these mass-market books makes it impractical to list them in our annotated bibliography.[5]

Some critics say that the inspirational romance does a disservice to Christian readers; they charge that this type of novel panders to the sensual desire that secular romance novels have always inflamed. They say the inspirational romance may cultivate the reader's desire for secular romances.

I must confess that I have not read enough books in this genre to comment intelligently on this criticism. But I would observe that the quality of writing in most inspirational romances tends to be far inferior to that of the biblical novel and other types of adult Christian fiction. The characters tend to be stereotyped, the plots are often mechanical, and the story's references to spiritual matters are often made in a perfunctory, superficial way. I suspect that in the next few years we will see more careful and skillful writing emerge in this category of Christian fiction, or it will pass from the scene as a fad.

As you can see, you have a variety of Christian novels and stories from which to choose. Christian fiction is a growing field of literature. One might say it is the missionary edge of Christian publishing today, since unbelievers are more likely to read a book of Christian fiction than a book of doctrine or Scripture exposition. The subtle gospel message of the Christian novel may hook their souls more easily than the earnest arguments of those other books.

And Christian fiction can awaken the imagination of a Christian reader. It can help you see the spiritual significance of the seemingly mundane events of your life. It can allow you to live vicariously in the shoes of people who are wrestling with life-and-death issues. Even if you never confront those issues

---

[4]Yvonne Lehman, "Writing the Inspirational Romance," *The Writer* (December 1984), p. 15.
[5]Mass-market paperback novels are usually sold through special retailing plans that require the bookseller to return any unsold copies within a few months. For this reason, a given title will seldom be kept in stock for more than a year.

personally, your friends may; if so, the Christian novel could prepare you to counsel those friends more intelligently.

We evangelical Christians have inherited a Puritan aversion to any sort of entertainment, whether it be the theater or TV or "light reading." Yet we should realize that well-written Christian fiction is more than "light reading." It helps us deal with the most basic matters of our faith in an experiential way, rather than a didactic or analytical way. We can derive great devotional benefit from reading the best Christian fiction and reflecting upon its realistic vignettes of life.

ANNOTATED BIBLIOGRAPHY

Buechner, Frederick. *Godric*. San Francisco: Harper and Row, 1983.

Godric is a historical novel about a real twelfth-century merchant seaman who became a Christian evangelist and poet. Godric's extraordinary life inspired countless legends in medieval England. Buechner has re-created this fascinating character with intriguing realism, which leads us to wonder where fact ends and where the fiction begins. But no matter how we slice it, *Godric* is an enlightening and well-crafted story.

Bunyan, John. *The Pilgrim's Progress*. Old Tappan NJ: Fleming H. Revell, 1965.[6]

Bunyan describes the Christian's spiritual journey toward heaven in terms of an allegory—the tale of a young, naive traveler named Christian who encounters many exciting and life-threatening incidents as he walks toward the fabled City of Light. The rich literary symbolism of this book has caused many public school teachers to use it in courses of English literature. Some people read the book several times, observing a different level of meaning each time they review it. *Pilgrim's Progress* has inspired scores of other Christian allegories.

Call, Max. *Phoebe*. Grand Rapids: Zondervan, 1980.

---

[6]Also available from Roger Sharrock, ed. (New York: Penguin, 1965), (New York: Airmont Publishing, 1968), (New Canaan CT: Keats, 1972), (Grand Rapids: Zondervan, 1973), (Laurel NY: Lightyear Press, 1976), (New York: Dodd, Mead, & Company, 1979), (Carlisle PA: The Banner of Truth, 1979), (Springdale PA: Whitaker House, 1981), (Ringgold LA: Bible Memory Association, 1981), Hal M. Helms, ed. (Orleans MA: Paraclete Press, 1982), (Chicago: Moody, 1984), (New York: Oxford University Press, 1984), (Grand Rapids: Baker, 1984); in an illustrated Spanish version titled *El Progreso del Peregrino Illustrado* from (Grand Rapids: Kregel, n.d.); as *Pilgrim's Progress: From This World to That Which Is to Come*, James B. Wharey and Roger Sharrock, eds. (New York: Oxford University Press, 1960); in a large-print edition from (New Canaan CT: Keats, 1983); as a simplified modern version suitable for reading to children by Jean Watson, *The Family Pilgrim's Progress* (Wheaton IL: Tyndale House, 1984); *Pilgrim's Progress in Today's English* from (Chicago: Moody, 1960); and as *Pictorial Pilgrim's Progress* from (Chicago: Moody, 1964).

Max Call bases this fascinating biblical novel on the premise that Phoebe, a young Christian businesswoman, was entrusted with Paul's epistle to the Christians in Rome. Her efforts to reach the capital city and deliver this crucial document will bring Phoebe into conflict with some strong-willed opponents of the church.

Giertz, Bo. *The Hammer of God*, trans. by Clifford A. Nelson. Minneapolis: Augsburg, 1973.

Three Swedish pastors encounter a morass of personal and pastoral problems that are far beyond their ability to cope. Each learns that he must rely on the grace of God for the guidance and strength to survive.

Henderson, Lois T. *Abigail*. San Francisco: Harper and Row, 1983.

Abigail was King David's wife who proved to be a wise woman and a skillful diplomat—especially when dealing with David's enemies. The latest of Lois Henderson's fine Bible-based novels about women, *Abigail* seems destined to become another favorite of Christian women readers.

Henderson, Lois T. *Hagar*. San Francisco: Harper and Row, 1983.

My wife greatly enjoyed this novel because it throws a more favorable light on the character of Hagar, Sarah's handmaid and (so it seemed) the rival for her husband's affections. The author reveals the customs of marriage and slavery that led to Hagar's predicament. And she considers how this young woman must have felt, trying to please her mistress in every way yet incurring her wrath when she did.

Henderson, Lois T. *Lydia*. San Francisco: Harper and Row, 1982.

Continuing her skillful retelling of the stories of Bible women, Lois Henderson turns to a New Testament figure who seems at first like many career women of today. Lydia, "the seller of purple" who assisted Paul in launching the Christian missionary effort in Europe, surely has a more complex personality than the slight references of Scripture might suggest. Henderson gives her a history and a character that is quite different from that of the stereotyped professional woman—but perhaps more like the real Christian women who work in the business world.

Henderson, Lois T. *Miriam*. San Francisco: Harper and Row, 1983.

Lois Henderson adds another choice volume to her series of Bible-based novels with this story of Miriam, sister of Moses and Aaron. The basic facts of the novel come directly from Scripture—Miriam's courageous leadership during the Exodus, her being named priestess, her siding with Aaron in an effort to usurp Moses' authority, and the humbling aftermath of that confrontation. Henderson imaginatively weaves these facts into an engrossing, colorful narrative that is exciting to read.

Henderson, Lois T. *Ruth*. San Francisco: Harper and Row, 1981.

The first (and, some say, the best) of Henderson's Bible-based novels, *Ruth* tells the story of this Old Testament woman with profound sensitivity and imagination. Henderson embellishes the narrative with colorful descriptions of the personalities, the often-changing location, and the dialogue. Yet at no point does she violate the scriptural report of Ruth's experience or the knowledge that modern researchers have gleaned about the customs of that day. This is a fascinating story that holds the reader's attention from first to last.

Hurnard, Hannah. *Hind's Feet on High Places*. Wheaton IL: Tyndale House, 1977.

Hurnard borrows a simile from Habakkuk 3:19, which says a servant of God shall overcome difficulties with grace and ease like that of "hind's feet on high places." This allegory is the story of a young woman named Much-Afraid, who is a servant of the Great Shepherd (representing Christ). Because of her deformities and past failures, Much-Afraid hesitates to do what her master says, for fear that she will fail again. She experiences many trying problems, as she attempts to reform herself, till she learns that her master has a better way of service.

Lewis, C. S. *The Chronicles of Narnia*, 7 vols. New York: Collier Books, 1970.

This boxed set of paperbacks includes all the tales from Lewis's well-known Narnia series: *The Lion, the Witch, and the Wardrobe*; *Prince Caspian*; *The Voyage of the "Dawn Treader"*; *The Silver Chair*; *The Horse and His Boy*; *The Magician's Nephew*; and *The Last Battle*. These fantasies revolve around the exploits of children who enter the enchanted world of Narnia, where the struggle between good and evil rages at full pitch. Children especially enjoy these fantasies, since children are the protagonists; and adults enjoy reading them, both for the religious significance and their sheer entertainment value.[7]

Lewis, C. S. *Pilgrim's Regress*. Grand Rapids: Eerdmans, 1958.

The title may suggest that this is a parody of Bunyan's classic allegory, *Pilgrim's Progress*; yet nothing could be farther from the truth. Lewis regards Bunyan's work with respect. In fact, he imitates it as a gesture of his respect—using a medieval kingdom peopled with knights, knaves, and clerics to depict his own early quest for Christian certitude. Lewis's book contains allegorical

---

[7]Also available as a 7-volume hardcover set from (New York: Macmillan, 1956).

symbols far more obscure than Bunyan's work. It will be better appreciated by those familiar with English history and literature, for they will better understand the significance of his symbols.

MacDonald, George. *The Fantasy Stories of George MacDonald*, 4 vols. Grand Rapids: Eerdmans, 1980.

MacDonald was a nineteenth-century British writer whose novels and fantasy stories influenced the fiction of C. S. Lewis, J. R. R. Tolkien, and Charles Williams. This set includes twenty of his most memorable stories, tastefully illustrated. They are suitable for reading to children; yet adults will appreciate the deep truths suggested by these overtly entertaining stories.

Marshall, Catherine. *Christy*. New York: Avon Books, 1967.

Christy Huddleston goes to the Smoky Mountains to teach school in a poverty-ridden community. Her youthful exuberance gives Christy a joyous outlook that ignores many of the problems she encounters; but she cannot ignore the challenge of the two men who try to win her heart. It's a challenge that tests her faith in God as well as her maturity as a woman.

Miller, Calvin. *The Singer*. Downers Grove IL: InterVarsity, 1975.

This is an allegory about a common laborer in medieval times who is so inspired by a certain melody that he resolves to become a traveling musician—a troubadour—who shares the music with others. Ridiculed by his friends and superiors, the singer must wrestle with his calling and the constraints of the society in which he lives. The publisher advertises this as "a delicate story in the tradition of C. S. Lewis and J. R. R. Tolkien," but I believe its allegorical symbols are more easily understood than theirs.[8]

Sheldon, Charles M. *In His Steps*. Grand Rapids: Baker, 1978.[9]

Sheldon imagines a nineteenth-century town that is radically transformed when the newspaper editor and other leading citizens begin to make each decision on the basis of a simple question: "What would Jesus do?" This is the most widely read Christian novel of modern times; it continues to hold a place on the religious best-seller lists though nearly a century has elapsed since its first publication.

---

[8]*The Singer* is the first in a trilogy that includes *The Song* (Downers Grove IL. InterVarsity: 1977) and *The Finale* (Downers Grove IL: InterVarsity: 1979).
[9]Also available from (New York: Putnam Publishing Group, 1982), (Westchester IL: Good News Publishers, 1962), (New Canaan CT: Keats, 1972), (Grand Rapids: Zondervan, 1977), (Fort Worth TX: Brownlow Publishing Co., 1982) in a large-print edition from (New Canaan CT: Keats, 1982); and in Spanish as *En Sus Pasos*, trans. by Ruth Reuben from (El Paso TX: Casa Bautista de Publicaiones, 1968).

Trollope, Anthony. *The Warden*. New York: Penguin Books, 1982.

First published in 1855, *The Warden* is a satire of the pompous hypocrisy that Trollope found in the Anglican Church of his day. It is the story of an honest and humble minister, Mr. Harding, warden of an almshouse for old men in the fictitious curacy of Bartsetshire. Harding becomes the victim—then the concerned observer—in his fellow clerics' struggles to obtain higher stations in the church. An entertaining yet arresting book, *The Warden* disarms our pride long enough to expose the flaws of our own churchly machinations.

vanDyke, Henry. *The Story of the Other Wise Man*. San Francisco: Harper and Row, 1983.

A reprint of vanDyke's 1895 classic, this book delights children as well as adults. Artaban, the main character, failed to reach his rendezvous with the other Magi in time to accompany them to Bethlehem. So he devotes the next thirty years of his life to an effort to find the Messiah. His quest is interrupted by many trials and diversions, through which Artaban learns a great deal about the way of life Jesus was teaching.

Wangerin, Walter, Jr. *Ragman and Other Cries of Faith*. San Francisco: Harper and Row, 1984.

Pastor of Grace Lutheran Church in Evansville, Indiana, Wangerin has created these realistic short stories from the observations of his pastoral ministry. Each story is brief yet deeply moving and vibrant with spiritual connotations.

Williams, Charles. *The Novels of Charles Williams*, 7 vols. Grand Rapids: Eerdmans, 1965–1981.

Williams's novels accept the reality of a supernatural order populated by angels and demons. Some deal with the torments and triumphs after death. These stories are graphically vivid, sometimes chilling, yet always devoted to portraying the conflict between God and Satan in which the Almighty is already victorious.

Chapter Seven
Books of Prayer

Roman Catholic Christians are well accustomed to using books of prayers approved by the church for their daily worship. These written prayers guide the Catholic worshiper through the traditional movements of adoration, confession, thanksgiving, and petition. Prayer books have become an indispensable part of Roman Catholic liturgy, and Catholic writers often create other books of informal prayers that are used for private devotions.

We cannot be sure where the practice of publishing prayer books began. Surely it is rooted deep in the tradition of the Western church. The great classical writers, such as Francis of Assisi and Bernard of Clairvaux, left us a rich legacy of written prayers used in their monastic devotional exercises. Yet the practice of meditating upon written prayers must antedate these medieval devotional writers.

In fact, we find many of the apostles' prayers recorded in the New Testament (Rom. 16:25-27; Phil. 1:8-11; Jude 24-25); and every serious Christian has pondered the truths of the Lord's Prayer, making it a model for his own prayer life (Luke 11:2-4). So we might say that written prayers have been a part of the devotional lives of Christians from the very beginning. Such prayers have inspired and instructed each generation of Christians in the practice of daily prayer.

Evangelical Protestants have tended to avoid the use of written prayers, perhaps because the prayer book is such a visible part of the Roman Catholic liturgy. But in recent years even the most conservative evangelicals have begun to discover the depth of spirituality in some books of prayers, which they are using as a guide for their own prayer life. One book of prayer used by Catholics and Protestants alike is John Baillie's *A Diary of Private Prayer* (New York: Charles Scribner's Sons, 1949). Because of Baillie's rootage in the Church of England, his work has been accepted by Christians from the sacramental and nonsacramental churches as well. In the preface to his classic book, Dr. Baillie says:

> These prayers are to be regarded as aids; they are not intended to form the whole of the morning's or evening's devotions or to take the place of more individual prayers for ourselves or others. On the blank left-hand pages such further petitions

and intercessions may be noted down. The prayers are suited to private use, not to the liturgical use of public worship.[1]

As Baillie's last comment suggests, he wrote the *Diary* as a devotional resource rather than a book for public worship. Its contents are more informal than one would find in the prayer books used in public worship; perhaps that is another reason for its wide popularity. Its readings flow with the naturalness of an individual Christian's quiet conversations with God, without any concern "to put on airs" or adopt a mood of affectation.

Baillie's *Diary* is but one example of the informal prayer books that modern Christians use in their private devotions. Other well-known contemporary books of prayer would include Michael Quoist's *Prayers* and *The Prayers of Peter Marshall*, edited by Catherine Marshall. As you can see, these books are being written by Christians from across the spectrum of worship traditions, just as they are being read and appreciated by all sorts of Christians.

How to Use Books of Prayer

If you do not use a prayer book in your times of public worship, you may feel a bit awkward when you first try to use one as the focus of your devotional meditations. Here are some suggested methods you could use to make a prayer book a resource for your daily devotional time:

1. Thought Starters. Read a prayer to orient yourself toward the act of prayer. Let the written prayer suggest the subject and attitude of your own prayer. In other words, when you begin praying pick up where the written prayer leaves off, expanding upon its ideas with petitions and praises of your own. You do not need to feel restricted by the written prayer. Your own prayer can range abroad to touch a wide field of concerns that the written prayer did not mention. Read the prayer with an open mind as if it were the spark that God will use to light the dry tinder of your soul.

Martin Luther customarily read the Ten Commandments and the Lord's Prayer during his daily devotions, taking one phrase at a time and enlarging upon it with his prayers. He felt that this guaranteed a well-rounded prayer experience, since these golden texts of Scripture encompass every aspect of a person's relationship with God. You might try something similar with a favorite passage of Scripture such as Psalm 23 or 1 Corinthians 13, taking one phrase at a time and reflecting upon its current significance for your life. Mold your prayer around the teachings of these Scriptures, and you may find yourself "thinking God's thoughts after him."

---

[1]John Baillie, *A Diary of Private Prayer* (New York: Charles Scribner's Sons, 1949), p. 7.

2. Models. As the Lord's Prayer is a model for every Christian, some modern written prayers can teach us how to shape our own prayers more thoughtfully. They may not use stilted formal language; in fact, they may seem conversational in tone. But if we study these prayers closely, we find that they trace a kind of map through the most important movements of prayer.

If we followed our usual impulses in prayer, we might dwell on petition and intercession, asking favors for ourselves and others. This is certainly an important aspect of prayer, as it demonstrates our utter dependence on God to provide the necessities and blessings of everyday life. But by no means are petition and intercession the core of prayer as Jesus taught it. Study the Lord's Prayer again. Study other model prayers from the devotional writers. You will discover that the "asking" movement of prayer is a minor theme in the individual's encounter with God; adoration, praise, and thanksgiving are the major themes. Perhaps by reading a model prayer in your daily devotional time, you will be reminded of your devotional priorities. If you imitate these model prayers, you may begin to look at the devotional time as an hour of intimate fellowship with God rather than as a bargaining session with him.

3. Revelations. The Bible says every Christian has times when he does not know how to pray (Rom. 8:26). Perhaps this is such a time for you. The tensions and anxieties of life so preoccupy your mind that you are distracted from the presence of the Lord. A recent experience with the Lord is so profound or puzzling that you do not know how to respond to him. Or perhaps your present needs are so acutely pressing that you do not know how to express them in a reverent, submissive manner. At such times, the Bible reassures us, the Holy Spirit intercedes with the Father on our behalf; he articulates our prayers even when we do not know what to say. When we are deadlocked in prayer, the Holy Spirit may use a written prayer to reveal to us the essence of our problem. He may also use a written prayer to help us begin articulating our deepest thoughts and feelings for ourselves, supplying the words that crystallize our ambient feelings into clear and understandable terms. Indeed, the Holy Spirit may use a written prayer to clarify our relationship with the Lord so that we can pray more intelligently and candidly. He can help us regain our voice, as it were, by showing us how someone in a similar predicament began to talk with God.

As you meditate upon a written prayer you may feel convicted of the wrongness of your attitudes toward God or your neighbor. If so, give thanks to the Lord for using this meditation to reveal your true state.

4. Liturgies. The word *liturgy* may be unfamiliar to you. It refers to a pattern for worship, normally the pattern used in a public worship service. I think that our private devotions have their own liturgy as well. That is, our own devotional time follows a certain routine of prayer, reading, meditation, praise, singing, and acts of service that express the fullness of our devotion to God.

And the reading of other people's prayers can be a meaningful part of our private devotional liturgy.

I visited a Roman Catholic retreat center where one wing of the facility was dedicated to silent prayer and meditation. This area was called Merton Hall in honor of the Roman Catholic monk Thomas Merton. A retreatant could live in the dormitory rooms of Merton Hall and spend his or her days communing with the Lord on the sunlit veranda or in the quietness of a small chapel. I noticed that prayer books were shelved in various locations in Merton Hall to encourage each retreatant to meditate on these prayers as a part of the meditation in solitude. These books were not intended for public worship but for private devotional study. I used them as part of my own devotional liturgy while I stayed at Merton Hall.

If the word *liturgy* still seems foreign to you, simply think of your pattern for private worship or your devotional habit. (I dislike using the word *routine* in connection with the devotional time, since it suggests going through the motions of worship in a thoughtless sort of way.) But whatever you choose to call your method of devotional practice, note that the reading of prayers can bring a refreshing change to what you do.

Besides the books listed in the annotated bibliography below, you will find some inspiring prayers in the journals (Chapter 9) and the spiritual classics (Chapter 2). You will find written prayers scattered throughout the books of poetry listed at the end of Chapter 5 as well.

ANNOTATED BIBLIOGRAPHY

Baillie, John. *A Diary of Private Prayer.* New York: Charles Scribner's Sons, 1949.

I have already explained that Baillie's book is a modern classic which has given both Catholics and Protestants a new appreciation for books of prayers. Each day's selection has a blank page facing it, so that the reader can record her or his own prayers for the day. So the *Diary* serves as a journal-keeping tool as well as an aid to private prayer.

Brandt, Leslie and Edith Brandt, *Growing Together: Prayers for Married People.* Minneapolis: Augsburg, 1975.

The name of Leslie Brandt is familiar to many as the author of a popular paraphrase of the Psalms. Here he and his wife offer eighty prayers that express the changing moods of marriage. It's an appropriate book for any married couple, young or old.

Chavis, Benjamin F., Jr. *Psalms from Prison.* New York: Pilgrim, 1983.

Chavis and nine other black activists were convicted in 1972 of inciting riots in Wilmington, NC. After ten years in various prisons, the Wilmington Ten were exonerated of these charges. Chavis's *Psalms* remind me of Martin Luther King's *Letter from the Birmingham Jail*—expressing faith in God's ultimate deliverance from the injustices of man.

Donne, John. *Devotions*. Ann Arbor: University of Michigan Press, 1959.[2]
   Written in 1623 while the famed poet was suffering a grave illness, these prayers reflect the progressive depths of a sick person's musing upon life and death. Donne's biographer Isaak Walton compared this book to a monument of the patriarchs, "who were wont to build their altars in that place where they had received their blessings."

Jones, Chris. *Lord, I Want to Tell You Something*. Minneapolis: Augsburg, 1973.
   A book of conversational prayers for boys aged eight to twelve, this book sets a pattern of frankness and intimacy with God that should last throughout life.

Kirk, James G. *When We Gather*. Philadelphia: Westminster, 1983.
   A collection of prayers to accompany Cycle A of the lectionary, this will be used most often in public services of worship. Yet the prayers have a vitality and felicity that make them good models for private prayer as well.

Klug, Lyn. *I Know I Can Trust You, Lord*. Minneapolis: Augsburg, 1983.
   Sixty conversational prayers are found in this compact book for girls aged eight to twelve. Illustrated with black-and-white photos, it makes a thoughtful yet inexpensive gift.

Luther, Martin. *Luther's Prayers*, ed. by Herbert F. Brokering, trans. by Charles E. Kistler. Minneapolis: Augsburg, 1967.
   The boldness and spiritual perceptiveness of the great Reformer is clearly evident in this small collection of his prayers. His doctrinal discernment is also seen. Perhaps no other book of prayers is so rich in its affirmation of scriptural truth.

Murphy, Elspeth C. *Chalkdust: Prayer Meditations for Teachers*. Grand Rapids: Baker, 1978.
   Few people lead more harried, pressured lives than teachers in our public schools. Murphy provides these time-pressed readers a book of brief model prayers to orient their thoughts for each day. The book has three sections: "Prayers for the Children," "Prayers for Special Times," and "Prayers for the Teacher."

---

[2]Also available from (Folcroft Library Editions, Folcroft PA, 1973).

Oglesby, Stuart R. *Prayers for All Occasions*. Atlanta: John Knox, 1940.

Containing prayers for everyday situations as well as special occasions, this little book continues to be popular more than forty-five years after its first publication. Oglesby was pastor of Central Presbyterian Church in Atlanta from 1930 to 1958. The prayers in his book are dignified, yet warm with the spirit of a pastor's devotion to Christ.

Parker, Joseph. *Joseph Parker Treasury of Pastoral Prayers*. Grand Rapids: Baker, 1982.

Parker was one of the foremost Methodist pastors of Great Britain, a gifted preacher and leader of public worship. This collection of his prayers could serve as a helpful model for those who lead prayer in public meetings today, as the introductory article by Stephen Olford suggests. But it also has great inspirational value for private study.

Quoist, Michael. *Prayers*, trans. by Agnes M. Forsyth and Anne Marie de Commaille. New York: Sheed and Ward, 1963.[3]

A collection of informal yet reverent prayers by a French Catholic, this book has been used by many Protestants as well. In fact, some Protestant ministers have adopted Quoist's prayers as part of their congregational order of worship. Simple, heartfelt expressions of one man's experience with the Lord.

Rahner, Karl. *Encounters with Silence*, trans. by James A. Demske. Westminster MD: The Newman Press, 1966.

Highly respected as professor of dogmatic theology at the University of Innsbruck, Austria, Dr. Rahner is accustomed to writing on a high level of theological sophistication. Not so with this book. A collection of simply worded prayers, *Encounters* will lead you through the soul-searching depths of a Christian's effort to understand who God is. The author is Roman Catholic, but his *Encounters* express the spiritual wrestlings of all devout Christians.

Sallee, Lynn. *Coffee Time Prayers*. Grand Rapids: Baker, 1976.

Written by a woman, this book clearly expresses the thoughts that crowd into the mind of a busy wife and mother when she has some time alone. These jumbled and sometimes conflicting thoughts are offered up to God for his blessing and direction. An honestly written book, it will strike a responsive note in the hearts of many women.

Savage, Robert C. *Pocket Prayers*. Wheaton IL: Tyndale House, 1982.

---

[3]Also available from (Andrews, McMeel, and Parker, Fairway KS, 1974).

Published as an inexpensive pocket-size paperback, this collection of 777 brief prayers can be a useful aid to Christians on the go. Savage is a retired Baptist minister.

Shepherd, J. Barrie. *Diary of Daily Prayer*. Minneapolis: Augsburg, 1975.
Shepherd gives us sixty prayers—thirty each for morning and evening—in the simple and humble spirit we would expect from this great Scottish Christian. A blank page opposite each prayer allows you to record your own prayers and thoughts on each day of this month-long journal experience.

Speiss, Margaret B. *Gather Me Together, Lord*. Grand Rapids: Baker, 1982.
Written especially for busy mothers, these prayers reflect the demands of housekeeping, child-rearing, and husband-pleasing that are sure to take their toll on modern moms. The book is filled with the kind of warmth, tenderness, and humor that can be a healing balm to a mother's heart.

Williams, Dick, ed. *Prayers for Today's Church*. Minneapolis: Augsburg, 1977.
Here is one of the largest collections of prayers for use in public worship. Containing nearly five hundred prayers, Williams's book offers something on virtually every conceivable theme of a worship service. It is especially good for its recognition of contemporary social problems.

Zundel, Veronica, ed. *Eerdman's Book of Famous Prayers*. Grand Rapids: Eerdmans, 1983.
Here is a colorful anthology of prayers uttered by Christians from every century. Augustine, Thomas Aquinas, Jonathan Edwards, Amy Carmichael, Blaise Pascal, Corrie ten Boom, and Mother Teresa are just a few of the memorable saints quoted here. Illustrated tastefully with full-color photographs and an eye-pleasing page design, this book makes an attractive gift.

Chapter Eight
Christian Biographies
and Autobiographies

David Brainerd was an early missionary among the American Indians when colonists began to push into the frontier. His harrowing experiences were recorded by the noted Massachusetts pastor Jonathan Edwards, who wrote *The Life of David Brainerd* not only to describe the difficulties of the American missionary enterprise, but to inspire the faith and courage of Christians in far less dangerous situations than Brainerd had encountered.

Edwards's biography of Brainerd was widely distributed in England, where it had a profound influence on John Wesley. Wesley published an inexpensive paperback edition of the book, which made its way into the homes of thousands of his Methodist friends. In the years to come, this book inspired William Carey, Hudson Taylor, Charles Cowman, and scores of other earnest Christians who answered the call to foreign missionary service.

Brainerd's biography is but one example of how powerfully the lives of our spiritual ancestors can influence our own faithfulness to the Lord. As Richard J. Foster says, "Many others have traveled the same path and have left markers."[1]

Testimony Books

I feel we should distinguish between standard Christian biography or autobiography and the popular genre known as "testimony books." Testimony books record the ebullient first impressions of a new Christian, written perhaps two or three years after conversion. These books are full of victory and hope, often marked with marvelous experiences of the grace of God. They can rally our own faith by reminding us of the delights we knew when we were still babes in Christ. I've listed several of these books in Chapter 3.

However, the Christian biography or autobiography reviews a much longer span of time. Not only does it record the defeats and victories of the subject's Christian life, but it reflects a marked degree of spiritual maturing which

---

[1]Richard J. Foster, *Celebration of Discipline* (San Francisco: Harper and Row, 1978), p. 63.

comes only after the passage of years and wrestling with the deep mysteries of God. Both the testimony book and the Christian biography have legitimate functions; each is an accurate record of the subject's experiences. But because of the biography's long-range focus and more careful analysis, I believe it has far greater value for the shaping of our lives.

Another important distinction should be made between an official or "authorized" biography and other types. An official biography has been written with the consent of the subject or the subject's family, so the author probably had access to private papers and personal interviews that would make this work more detailed and accurate. Other biographies may be written without consulting the subject or the family; but they have the perspective of an outside observer peering into the fishbowl of the subject's life. Typically, they do not have the warmth and intimacy, much less the factual accuracy, that an official biography can provide. If you read the cover advertisement or the preface of a biography, you can learn whether it is an authorized work; and this will help you decide whether it is worth your time, especially if several biographies about this person are available. (Examples of persons who are the subjects of several unofficial biographies are Billy Graham, Dwight L. Moody, and Billy Sunday.)

Biography and Hagiography

Early church historians such as Eusebius wrote biographies of Christian martyrs and church leaders that were embellished with fanciful legend. Though these epic stories were thrilling, they could not be proved as fact. This kind of embroidered stories of the saints, commonly called *hagiography*, was the most common kind of Christian biography until the time of *Foxe's Book of Martyrs*.

But over the last two centuries Christian readers have demanded a more careful handling of the facts, even in biographies of the most revered saints. We enjoy the inspiration and the thrill of reading about the adventures of God's heroes and heroines, but we want to be sure that we get a realistic picture of what they did. Modern Christian biographies are likely to be much more accurate in this regard.

Special Types

In the 1950s and 1960s Christian publishers produced dozens of missionary biographies, since that was a time of missionary expansion after World War II. Youth biographies (that is, biographies in simple language for teenagers) were also popular during those two decades. Both the missionary biography and the youth biography have declined in popularity, to be replaced by biographies of noted Christian thinkers, such as *Malcolm Muggeridge: A Life*, by Ian Hunter (Thomas Nelson, 1980); *John R. Mott: A Biography*, by C. Howard Hopkins (Eerdmans, 1979); and *Treasure in Clay: The Autobiography of Fulton J. Sheen*, by Fulton J. Sheen (Doubleday, 1980). I believe we will see many more biographies of evangelical thinkers in the next decade as prominent figures like Francis Schaeffer, Billy Graham, Carl F. H. Henry, and Frank Gaebelein come to the end of their careers.

Some Christian publishers have given special attention to so-called celebrity "biographies" in recent years. These are actually testimony books about the conversion experiences of well-known public figures such as Charles Colson, B. J. Thomas, Barbara Mandrell, John DeLorean, and others. While these books attract an avid group of readers, these books seem to have limited devotional value because they are based on such a short span of the subject's Christian experience. One is always glad to see a person come to accept Jesus as Lord, and perhaps the passage of time will prove a celebrity's faithfulness to the Lord. Meanwhile I believe the life stories of Christian people outside the limelight of public acclaim will have the most enduring value as models for our faith.

ANNOTATED BIBLIOGRAPHY

Allen, Diogenes. *Three Outsiders*. Cambridge MA: Cowley Publications, 1983.

For those interested in studying some unorthodox figures in the history of devotional writing, this book offers three—Blaise Pascal, Soren Kierkegaard, and Simone Weil. All chose to stand outside the institutional church and challenge the Christian traditions of their day; yet all were intensely interested in learning how to live a God-honoring life. Professor Allen of Princeton Theological Seminary examines this devotional aspect of the otherwise controversial lives of these "outsiders."

Bacon, Ernest W. *John Bunyan: Pilgrim and Dreamer*. Grand Rapids: Baker, 1984.

The courageous seventeenth-century Puritan John Bunyan has endeared himself to generations of Christians with his allegorical novels, especially *The Pilgrim's Progress*. Yet few readers know the facts of Bunyan's own torturous pilgrimage, which included imprisonment and poverty for the sake of his Christian convictions. Bacon has done us a great service by bringing the details of Bunyan's life before us once again. It is a story to thrill and convict us concerning our own commitment to God.

Barclay, William. *William Barclay: A Spiritual Autobiography*. Grand Rapids: Eerdmans, 1977.

Barclay's *Daily Study Bible* commentary has introduced thousands of lay-persons to a more serious study of God's Word. Now he sets down the story of his whole ministry, which included lecturing on the British Broadcasting Corporation and other innovative ways of reaching the English-speaking world with the gospel.

Bunyan, John. *Grace Abounding to the Chief of Sinners*. New York: Oxford University Press, 1966.[2]

Though not as well known as *Pilgrim's Progress*, this work by Bunyan describes his own tortuous path to Christ and the many trials that he endured as a street preacher. Often imprisoned and ridiculed for his faith, Bunyan still rejoiced that God gave him sufficient grace to continue his gospel ministry. This might be called his spiritual autobiography. Its plain language and soul-searching courage still speaks to Christians.

Carter, Jimmy. *Why Not the Best?* Nashville: Broadman, 1975.

Governor Jimmy Carter wrote this autobiography in the early months of his campaign for the presidency in 1976. It forthrightly declares his Christian convictions on matters of conscience as well as matters of politics. One wishes the book were updated to cover President Carter's term in the White House and his subsequent years of retirement. Nonetheless the book allows us to see the rising career of a key evangelical leader.

Cecil, Richard. *The Life of John Newton*. Grand Rapids: Baker, 1978.

Newton's hymns are familiar to any Western Christian. Virtually every modern hymnal contains his work. But few know the torment of soul that Newton endured as a slave trader whom God began convicting and drawing to the point of conversion. Cecil's biography reveals the man in his sorrow and his joy.

Colson, Charles. *Born Again*. Grand Rapids: Zondervan, 1976.[3]

Colson was President Nixon's chief legal counsel during the Watergate scandal. Reporters called him Nixon's "hatchet man" because of his brusque manner in dealing with political enemies. But in the midst of the Watergate crisis, God convicted Colson of his sins and brought him to a painful surrender to Christ. He was tried and convicted of his crimes, yet publicly testified of his new allegiance to Christ. *Born Again* is Colson's firsthand account of the complete turnaround that God made of his life.

---

[2] Also available from Baker, (Grand Rapids, 1978) and (Biblio Distribution Center, Totowa NJ, 1979).
[3] Also available from Fleming H. Revell, (Old Tappan NJ, 1977) and in Spanish as *Naci de Nuevo*, Rhode Ward, trans. from (Miami FL: Editorial Caribe, 1977).

Dale, Alzina Stone. *The Outline of Sanity: A Life of G. K. Chesterton.* Grand Rapids: Eerdmans, 1982.

Chesterton was a gifted essayist and short story writer who expressed his Christian convictions in the sophisticated intellectual arena of Great Britain two generations ago. This portrait of Chesterton will give you a new appreciation of the personal struggles that shaped his faith, as well as the criticism he received from other members of the intelligentsia.

Douglas, W. M. *Andrew Murray and His Message.* Grand Rapids: Baker, 1981.

Elsewhere in this book (especially Chapters 2 and 3) I have referred you to some of Murray's choice devotional and inspirational works. His biography is no less inspiring. Though often criticized for his connections with the Keswick Convention and his bold political views, Murray challenged the faith of millions through his sermons, lectures, and meditative books.

Edwards, Jonathan. *The Life of David Brainerd,* Norman Pettit, ed. New Haven CT: Yale University Press, 1984.

Brainerd was a brave missionary to the American Indians in the early 1700s, a man who learned to trust God for his security and provision in the midst of very hostile situations. Edwards's biography of Brainerd captured the imagination of American colonists and British Christians (including John Wesley), challenging them to trust more fully in God's protective care. It continues to be one of the most widely read of all Christian biographies. This edition of the biography is volume 7 of the series, *The Works of Jonathan Edwards.*

Elliot, Elisabeth. *Through Gates of Splendor.* Wheaton IL: Tyndale House, 1981.

Jim Elliot, Elisabeth's husband, landed with a planeload of missionaries in a remote jungle area of Amazonia where they were massacred by fierce Auca Indians. Mrs. Elliot tells the story of that ill-fated mission trip with excerpts from Jim's letters and his diary. She also tells the marvelous aftermath of the massacre, as she returned to the Aucas and led many of them to Jesus Christ—including the men who murdered her husband.

Fant, David J. *A. W. Tozer: A Twentieth Century Prophet.* Camp Hill PA: Christian Publications, 1964.

Tozer is a familiar name to readers of modern inspirational books. A prolific writer and noted editor of *The Alliance Weekly,* Tozer condemned half-hearted Christianity and exhorted fellow Christians to more disciplined and committed living. Fant's biography traces his career as pastor, evangelist, editor, and author.

Finney, Charles G. *An Autobiography*. Old Tappan NJ: Fleming H. Revell, 1966.[4]

Charles Finney exerted a powerful influence upon the Christian world of the 1800s. Formerly an attorney, Finney experienced a dramatic conversion to Jesus Christ and became a minister. He was one of the first to issue an "altar call" at the end of his sermons, making a forthright appeal for his listeners to be saved. Finney eventually became president of Oberlin College, where he astounded the religious world by urging radical reforms such as the abolition of slavery. His *Autobiography* traces the life story of one of the world's most sensitive and passionate Christian reformers.

Foxe, John. *Foxe's Book of Martyrs*, W. Grinton Berry, ed. Grand Rapids: Baker, 1978.[5]

A *martyr* is a person whose life and death bears witness to the saving power of Jesus Christ. In this old classic of religious biography, Foxe reviews the martyrdom of many leaders from the apostolic and ante-Nicene eras of church history. It makes gruesome reading, and modern church historians question the reliability of Foxe's data at many points; yet it should be read in light of the persecution that Christians continue to suffer around the world. No Christian knows when she or he might be called to martyrdom as well.

Furlong, Monica. *Merton: A Biography*. New York: Harper and Row, 1980.

Furlong's official biography of Thomas Merton is clearly the most definitive study of this important twentieth-century Catholic writer. After several years of trying to break into the literary circles of New York, Merton entered the Genesee monastery in Kentucky, where he might have spent the remainder of his life in contemplation. By an unusual turn of events, he published his spiritual autobiography, *The Seven-Storey Mountain*, and gained widespread recognition as an incisive devotional writer. Furlong draws upon many of his letters and private notes to compile a portrait of this formative figure.

Guyon, Jeanne Marie Bouviere de la Mothe. *The Autobiography of Madame Guyon*, trans. by Thomas Taylor Allen. New Canaan CT: Keats, 1980.[6]

Ruth Bell Graham calls this "a strange autobiography, deeply inspiring, at times disturbing." Madame Guyon was a French noblewoman of the court of Louis XIV, an intense mystic and a counselor of passionate involvement. Like Fenélon, she advised her friends to remain faithful to Jesus Christ despite the gross materialism of their day. Her unusual visions and her boldness in con-

---

[4]Also available from Helen S. Wessel, ed. (Minneapolis: Bethany House, 1977).
[5]Also available from Fleming H. Revell, (Old Tappen NJ, 1981).
[6]Another translation is available from Moody, (Chicago, n.d.).

fronting men of power earned Madame Guyon a permanent place in secular history, as well as the history of Christian spirituality.

Hopkins, C. Howard. *John R. Mott: A Biography*. Grand Rapids: Eerdmans, 1979.

Mott earnestly desired to see greater cooperation among the various Christian communions of the world. "It has been my ever present ambition to do something for the world," he wrote. He fulfilled this ambition as he directed the Student Christian Movement, helped shape the World Council of Churches, and built bridges of ecumenical cooperation in other ways. Hopkins has written a superb biography of this important twentieth-century leader, a biography so meticulously researched and painstakingly written that it should serve as a model for other Christian biographers.

Houghton, Frank. *Amy Carmichael of Dohnavur*. Fort Washington PA: Christian Literature Crusade, 1974.

Houghton perceptively traces the difficult missionary career of Amy Carmichael, who served over fifty-five years among the orphans and other needy souls of India. The last two decades of her life were fraught with illness; yet, in the very midst of her suffering, Miss Carmichael wrote some of the most moving inspirational literature to come from the Indian field. This biography depicts the true greatness of this spiritual heroine, recognizing that all of her strength and success came from her Lord.

Jones, E. Stanley. *A Song of Ascents: A Spiritual Autobiography*. Nashville: Abingdon, 1968.

Written when Jones was eighty-three, *A Song of Ascents* lacks the richness of detail that Jones's life story deserves. Yet what Jones lacks in reporting the facts he overcomes with a tender recollection of his feelings. This is an intimate biography—one might say, a book of confessions. And perhaps that is more suited to Jones himself, a gentle man who responded to difficulties with kindness, patience, and a willingness to trust God.

Keller, W. Phillip. *Wonder O' the Wind*. Waco TX: Word, 1982.

Keller tells his life story from the trying and often tragic years as a youngster on the mission compound in Kenya to his active ministry of teaching and writing devotional books. If you have been blessed by Keller's devotional expositions such as *A Shepherd Looks at the Twenty-Third Psalm* and *Lessons from a Sheepdog*, you will enjoy getting better acquainted with the author.

Kerr, Hugh T. and John M. Mulder, eds. *Conversions: The Christian Experience*. Grand Rapids: Eerdmans, 1983.

This is a collection of the first-person accounts of the conversions of fifty well-known Christians, ranging from Augustine to Charles Colson. The editors provide a thumbnail sketch of each person's life, followed by a brief excerpt in that writer's own words of how she or he came to Jesus Christ. This fascinating collection of testimonies well conveys the fervor and triumph of these people's conversion experiences.

Kinnear, Angus I. *Against the Tide: The Story of Watchman Nee*. Fort Washington PA: Christian Literature Crusade, 1973.

Many have written stirring articles about the dramatic life of Chinese evangelist Watchman Nee (1903–72), who actively preached and pastored churches in mainland China during the Sino-Japanese War, World War II, and under the Communist regime of Mao Tse-tung. This is a story full of miracles—perhaps the greatest being Watchman's persistent faith in the face of seeming insuperable problems.

Lambert, D. W. *An Unbribed Soul*. Fort Washington PA: Christian Literature Crusade, 1968.

This brief yet colorful biography of Oswald Chambers will fascinate the many readers of Chambers's popular devotional books. Though we know him best as author of *My Utmost for His Highest*, Chambers had a distinguished career as a missionary to Japan and Egypt and as a Bible teacher in England and the United States. *An Unbribed Soul* gives us a fuller appreciation of his vigorous life. An annotated bibliography of Chambers's books is included.

Lewis, C. S. *Surprised by Joy*. New York: Harcourt, Brace, and World, 1956.

Lewis was a distinguished professor of English literature at Oxford, a confirmed skeptic toward the Christian message until a peculiar sequence of events led him to reevaluate Christ's claims upon his life. This spiritual autobiography explains how Lewis found true joy and intellectual certitude through surrendering his life to Jesus.

Loveland, John. *Blessed Assurance: The Life and Hymns of Fanny J. Crosby*. Nashville: Broadman, 1978.

The hymns of this blind songwriter continue to appear as standard selections in the hymnals of virtually every evangelical church. Loveland's book not only recounts the events of Crosby's life, but examines the basic convictions of this woman who has enabled millions of Christians to articulate their faith in music.

Ludwig, Charles. *Sankey Still Sings*. Grand Rapids: Baker, 1981.

Ira Sankey was D. L. Moody's song leader and the composer of many revival tunes that are still sung today. Ludwig recounts the musician's life with imaginative flair. It's an interesting book for teens as well as adults.

Marshall, Catherine. *Meeting God at Every Turn*. Grand Rapids: Zondervan, 1981.[7]

Wife of the colorful Presbyterian preacher and Senate chaplain Peter Marshall, the author has given us many cherished inspirational books such as *Adventures in Prayer* and *Beyond Our Selves*. This is Mrs. Marshall's spiritual autobiography, a joyous affirmation of God's care throughout the tests and triumphs of her busy public life.

Merton, Thomas. *The Seven-Storey Mountain*. Garden City NY: Garden City Books, 1951.

Critics have hailed this as one of the great Christian books of the century. Conservative readers, Catholic and Protestant, are reluctant to endorse Merton's work because he later expressed an eclectic fondness for Buddhism and other non-Christian religions. Yet *The Seven-Storey Mountain* should be valued as a candid apologetic of a man who turned from secularism to Christianity. It is all the more valuable because Merton was persuaded to accept Christ and his claims as a result of prayer and contemplative study, a pilgrimage most unusual in this skeptical age.

Newman, Cardinal John Henry. *Apologia Pro Vita Sua*. Garden City NY: Doubleday, 1956.[8]

This spiritual autobiography by one of the great Roman Catholic leaders of the nineteenth century reveals the struggles and doubts that typically plague a new Christian's life. Candid and heartfelt, Newman's book has encouraged many who seek the assurance of God's love.

Oates, Stephen B. *Let the Trumpet Sound: The Life of Martin Luther King, Jr.* New York: New American Library, 1982.

William Manchester, the official biographer of President Kennedy, calls this "*the* book on Martin Luther King." Oates recounts the tumultuous events of this Christian reformer's efforts to win equal rights for black people. A Southern Baptist minister, Dr. King engaged the forces of bigotry with a true prophet's authority and zeal. Oates's book is thoroughly researched, colorfully written, and candid in its assessment of King's lasting impact on Ameri-

---

[7]Also available from Fleming H. Revell, (Old Tappen NJ, n.d.).

[8]Also available from David De Laura, ed. (New York: W. W. Norton & Co., 1968) and as *Apologia Pro Vita Sua: Being a History of His Religious Opinions*, Martin J. Svaglic, ed. (New York: Oxford University Press, 1967).

can society. One wishes he had devoted more attention to King's impact on the evangelical church.

Oates, Wayne E. *The Struggle to Be Free*. Philadelphia: Westminster, 1983.

Oates has earned his reputation as one of the foremost Christian counselors of our time. His spiritual autobiography is unique in two ways. First, it reflects on the psychological as well as the spiritual forces that affected Oates's life. Second, it explains how the reader can reflect on her or his own life story to gain insight for more faithful living.

Pierson, Arthur T. *George Müller of Bristol*. Old Tappan NJ: Fleming H. Revell, 1971.[9]

Müller had a remarkable ministry of caring for orphans at a complex of homes that he built in Bristol, England. The most remarkable aspect of his work was that he operated entirely by faith, praying that God would provide each material need at the appropriate time. Pierson's biography of this courageous man is full of miracle stories—modern miracles that remind us of what God can do in answer to prayer.

Pollock, John. *Amazing Grace: The Dramatic Life Story of John Newton*. San Francisco: Harper and Row, 1983.

Pollock carefully researched Newton's own handwritten journals and a wealth of other historical documents to write this fascinating biography. Newton wrote many of our best-loved hymns, including "Amazing Grace." The story of his life—how God reached him while he was a sea captain immersed in the slave trade—is indeed a testament to God's amazing grace.

Pollock, John. *Moody: The Biography*, rev. ed. Chicago: Moody, 1984.

Moody was the most dynamic Christian evangelist of the late nineteenth century. The fruit of his labor continues to bless Christians today as a result of the pioneering of thousands of pastors, teachers, and missionaries who were won to Christ through Moody's labors. Pollock has compiled the most thorough biography of Moody available. It is well-researched and delightful to read.

Reid, W. Stanford. *Trumpeter of God*. Grand Rapids: Baker, 1982.

This dramatic biography portrays the life of John Knox, the Scottish reformer who challenged the religious establishment and gave birth to the mod-

---

[9]Also available from Zondervan (Grand Rapids, 1984).

ern Presbyterian church. A bold yet troubled man, Knox deserves to bc better known by Christians today.

Sheen, Fulton J. *Treasure in Clay: The Autobiography of Fulton J. Sheen.* Garden City NY: Doubleday, 1980.

Biship Sheen emerged as one of America's first "electronic preachers" when he became the regular speaker for "The Catholic Hour," aired by the NBC radio network beginning in March 1930. In 1951 he began a weekly television series, "Life Is Worth Living," which eventually reached an audience of about thirty million. Through his broadcasts, newspaper columns, and books, he did more to reach the masses than any other American Catholic leader of this century. His autobiography is written in the breezy, informal, yet earnest style that endeared him to so many.

Spurgeon, Charles H. *Autobiography*, 2 vols. Carlisle PA: Banner of Truth, 1975–76.

A central figure in nineteenth-century evangelicalism, Charles Spurgeon continues to influence Christians through his profound sermons and devotionals. Here he tells his life story in his own modest words. A large and expensive work, but well worth the price for those who are eager to learn at the feet of one of the foremost evangelists of the Western world.

ten Boom, Corrie. *The Hiding Place*. Old Tappan NJ: Fleming H. Revell, 1974[10]

Miss ten Boom was a Dutch Christian whose family hid Jews from the Nazis in World War II. When their secret was discovered, the entire family was arrested and sent to several concentration camps. Corrie and her sister Betsy were sent to one of the worst, Auschwitz, where thousands were slaughtered or starved to death. Corrie struggled with feelings of anger and resentment toward God, but Betsy stayed true to the Lord to the moment she died. In this gripping account of those prison years, Corrie tells how her own faith rose from the ashes of the grim ordeal.

Teresa of Avila. *The Autobiography of St. Teresa of Avila*, trans. by E. Allison Peers. Garden City NY: Doubleday, 1960.

Teresa puzzled many of her contemporaries when she described the marvelous visions of heaven that she received at the height of her mystical devotions. She wrote this book to explain her spiritual pilgrimage and her hunger to be perfected in Christ. Modern readers are often perplexed by this story; yet it re-

---

[10]Also available from Bantam (New York, 1974).

mains the best account of the life of this visionary mystic.

Wiersbe, Warren W. *Victorious Christians You Should Know*. Grand Rapids: Baker, 1984.

The popular host of radio's "Back to the Bible" program compiled these life sketches of twenty outstanding Christians, many of whom are unfamiliar to modern readers. Everyone has heard of Fanny Crosby, J. Hudson Taylor, and Oswald Chambers; but you may not know the life stories of Katherine Luther, William Borden, Andrew Bonar, and other key figures in this book.

Chapter Nine
Journals and Journal Keeping

When I mention the word *diary* you might be inclined to think of a young girl keeping a private book in which she records the roller coaster emotions and outlandish fantasies of her youthful days—a book of personal confessions reserved for her eyes alone. Many of us got acquainted with the idea of journal keeping in just such a way by recording a diary during our youthful years when we found it awkward to talk with other people about the struggles within us. If we were to look back at those juvenile reflections we might feel embarrassed, even appalled, by some of the ideas we had the temerity to put on paper. But the embarrassment itself would indicate how much we have matured and how the act of keeping a diary helped us mature.

Journal keeping is not only for the young, however. Christian saints involved in the most trying kinds of service have recorded their experiences in journals. John Wesley is a good example. For some sixty years he kept a detailed journal of his ministry and thoughts which he published in several thick volumes before his death in 1792. Wesley's journals are still reprinted and widely circulated as a source of spiritual refreshment for pastors, evangelists, and others who are embroiled in the heat of servant ministry.

Yet the diaries of lesser known people can reveal as great a depth of spiritual reflection. One thinks of the diary of Anne Frank, a young Jewish girl who spent the last months of her life hiding from the Nazis and who confided her personal life aspirations to her diary. Though a young girl, Anne Frank reveals a great deal of maturity in the words of her diary. No doubt the act of keeping a diary aided her maturing; it forced her to analyze the significance of her tragic experience. Anne Frank died in one of Hitler's camps. But thousands of others have profited from reading Anne Frank's diary; they have grown as they have eavesdropped on the private meditations of this young girl.

At the end of this chapter I have listed the journals of some well-known Christians that may prove to be good resources for your devotional reading. Obviously, none of these books was written for publication, so their quality and style will vary. But I believe we can derive several benefits from reading them:

Candor. Because these journals were intended to be private, their comments about the difficulties of Christian living, the mysteries of God's will, and the disappointments of personal relationships are quite candid and without pretense. Too often an author's devotional or inspirational writings gloss over the difficult questions of his or her faith. But in a journal that same author may wrestle with those difficulties—even admit being stumped by them—and thus give us a better appreciation of our own spiritual difficulties.

Chronology. A Christian's journal may record progressive stages of a spiritual ordeal, showing how the writer came to a new understanding of his or her predicament over several weeks of praying and meditating about it. Spiritual insight seldom comes the first time we seek it, but after weeks and months of groping for the truth. A Christian's journal can reveal that process of groping, seizing partial answers, and groping yet again until the truth is grasped. This chronology of spiritual growth can reassure us during the times we feel frustrated with our own groping after God's will.

Clarity. I enjoy the journal of an articulate Christian thinker such as Wesley, who may turn quite an erudite phrase in more doctrinal writings but who comes right to the point (sometimes brutally so) in his journal entries about issues of theological debate and the persons involved in that debate. Stripped of all literary courtesies the theologian's journal is easy to understand, even to a greater degree than the same writer's letters. In fact, I would much prefer to get acquainted with a Christian thinker's ideas through his journals (if they are available) and then proceed to reading his polished, closely-marshalled arguments that were intended for publication. I am more likely to get an unadorned presentation of his ideas through the journal.

Journal Keeping

Besides the benefits of reading the published journals of these spiritual giants, we can aid our own spiritual growth by keeping a journal of our prayers and meditations each day. Such a journal might take the form of a one-paragraph summary of our activities and thoughts; it might be a more detailed report of a key event from each day; or it might be a rather lengthy essay-like commentary about some problem that is confronting us. We need not feel bound to follow a certain form. We can use whatever method seems most natural and useful in guiding our personal reflection.

Sam Keen has published some rather novel entries from his spiritual journal, which include dialogues between him and his emotions such as fear and anger.[1] This proved to be a useful way of coming to grips with the troublesome feelings that stirred within him. You might try a similar method of dealing with your emotions on paper.

Review your journal entries from time to time to see what you can learn

---

[1]Sam Keen, *To a Dancing God* (New York: Harper and Row, 1970), p. 109 ff.

from your experiences. You may be surprised to see the growth that is recorded on those pages. Richard J. Foster comments:

A journal is immensely encouraging, for we often forget over the years from what petty self-centered depths God has brought us. We tend to be so immersed in the tussle of the moment that we fail to see that the issues over which we now struggle are vastly more significant and substantial. Many matters are settled and behind us.

Beyond this, a journal has the added merit of focusing and concentrating our thinking. Writing out our concerns helps to clarify things and keeps us honest.[2]

If the discipline of keeping a daily journal seems a bit intimidating, you might try keeping a journal for a short, predetermined period of time such as on a weekend retreat. The results may encourage you to try keeping a spiritual journal for a longer period. If not, at least you will learn from the experience how to record your thoughts and feelings on paper.

Some Christians have begun sharing their spiritual journals with others in small prayer support groups, where they read brief excerpts that describe their current dealings with the Lord. Out of this sharing, they are able to pray more compassionately for one another. If the idea of sharing an intimate journal with a group of people seems too intimidating to you, try doing it with a single prayer partner whom you trust. The mere act of sharing what you have observed of your own life will make you accountable for change. It may prod you to take definite steps toward abandoning bad habits and cultivating more responsible ones.

ANNOTATED BIBLIOGRAPHY

Brainerd, David. *David Brainerd's Personal Testimony*. Grand Rapids: Baker, 1978.

Brainerd's own diary tells the story of his work among the American Indians in 1743–47. A book full of drama and inspiration, though not as well known as Jonathan Edwards's biography of this sainted missionary.

Elliott, Elisabeth. *The Journals of Jim Elliott* Old Tappan NJ: Fleming H. Revell, 1978.

Jim Elliott piloted a small plane that ferried missionaries into the jungles of the Amazon. Despite the high risks involved in this work, Elliott was delighted to employ his enthusiasm for flying in a full-time Christian ministry. These selections from his diary reveal the joys and occasionally the heartaches

---

[2]Richard J. Foster, *Freedom of Simplicity* (San Franciso: Harper and Row, 1981), pp. 108–9.

of his missionary work up to the day in 1956 when he and his comrades were massacred by a band of hostile Auca Indiana. Mrs. Elliott quoted some portions of this diary in her best-selling missionary biography, *Through Gates of Splendor*. I believe this edition of the *Journals* reveals even more of the humanness of her husband, who is honored as a modern Christian martyr.

John XXIII, Pope. *Journal of a Soul*, trans. by Dorothy White. New York: McGraw-Hill, 1965.

The most innovative pope of the twentieth century, John XXIII convened the dramatic council popularly known as "Vatican II," which called the Roman Catholic Church to seek greater concord with Christians of other traditions while revitalizing its own dogma and liturgy. John XXIII was more than a shrewd ecclesiastical leader; his journals reveal a man of sincere piety and open-mindedness. These published journals were begun when he was fourteen and continue until six months before his death. Suzanne Muto says, "His journal helps the reader to understand how the simple peasant boy achieved the greatness, the love of humanity, and the interior spiritual strength that invigorated his pontificate and inaugurated an era of reform and renewal within the Church."[3]

Kelsey, Morton T. *Adventure Inward*. Minneapolis: Augsburg, 1980.

One of the best books on Christian journal keeping. Kelsey explains step-by-step how to keep a useful record of each day's activities, thoughts, and impressions from God. He suggests how this journal can be used for self-assessment and spiritual growth.

Klug, Ronald. *How to Keep a Spiritual Journal*. Nashville: Thomas Nelson, 1982.

Here is a superb introduction to the practice of journal keeping. If you would like to try keeping a spiritual journal, I recommend that you start by reading Klug's book. He explains the benefits of journaling and leads you step-by-step through the process. Important advantages of this book are Klug's clear writing style and his crisp organization of instructions. They make this an excellent "how-to" book.

L'Engle, Madeleine. *A Circle of Quiet*. Minneapolis: Seabury Press, 1972.

L'Engle is a noted author and lecturer who yet finds time for solitude and

---

[3]Suzanne Muto, *A Guide to Spiritual Reading* (Denville NJ: Dimension Books, 1979), p. 186.

meditation at her Connecticut farm home, "Crosswicks." This book distills the observations from her daily journals there, blending humor and solemn reflection in a record of her spiritual growth.[4]

My Devotional Diary. Grand Rapids: Baker, 1976.
  This blank book can be used to record your thoughts, prayers, and aspirations from each day's devotional time.

Wesley, John. *The Journal of John Wesley*, Percy L. Parker, ed. Chicago: Moody, 1974.
  The Methodist Church began through the efforts of Wesley, who preached on street corners and open fields throughout England, calling nominal Christians to revival. Wesley did not intend to create a new denomination; he wanted to revive the Anglican Church. Yet the Anglican hierarchy opposed Wesley's efforts and soon after his death a separate church was organized. The *Journal* records Wesley's passionate ministry, his recurring confrontations with other Christian leaders (including his brother Charles), and his personal reflections on the state of Christianity in his times. Wesley published several editions of the *Journal* before his death in 1791.

Whitefield, George. *George Whitefield's Journals.* Carlisle PA: Banner of Truth, 1978.
  Whitefield was one of the greatest evangelists of modern times; he popularized the practice of open-air preaching during the evangelical revivals of the eighteenth century. A close friend of the Wesley brothers and other key figures of that era, he recorded in his journal a wealth of personal observations that help us understand how God used these leaders to alter the course of Western Christianity. Important for its inspirational quality as well as its historical interest.

---

[4]*A Circle of Quiet* is the first in a series called "The Crosswicks Journal Books." As the *Resource Guide* goes to press, three of these books have been issued. In addition to *A Circle of Quiet*, they are: *The Summer of the Great-Grandmother* (Minneapolis: Seabury, 1974) and *The Irrational Season* (Minneapolis: Seabury, 1977).

Chapter Ten
Discipleship Resources

As we discussed in Chapter 1, spiritual growth is not merely an individual matter. Christians grow together. In groups the Lord speaks through each member to encourage and prod us toward much deeper levels of spiritual maturity.

Since the early 1970s many Christians have begun meeting in discipleship groups. These usually begin when one Christian senses a need for help in the long and often discouraging life of "growing into the fullness of Christ" (Eph. 4:13). Such a person seeks out another Christian who is trusted to be more mature in the faith, a Christian with whom confidences can be shared and who can give some counsel in the week-by-week struggles of spiritual growth. The two make a covenant to meet regularly, perhaps once a week, to study the Bible and pray together as they share their current experiences in the Christian life. Over the course of time a discipleship pattern emerges in which the more mature Christian suggests a regimen of devotional exercises and service experiences through which the younger Christian can "try his or her wings."

The pair check over their progress in these areas of discipleship each time they meet—pointing out areas of weakness, praising one another at points of strength, and seeking the Lord's will for future growth. After a period of time, perhaps two or three years, the younger Christian feels ready to seek out another, younger disciple and form a discipleship bond with that person, meeting on a regular basis as he or she did with his or her mentor. This can evolve into a discipleship group of several dozen persons. Though the one-to-one sharing continues, the discipling pairs meet together for group Bible study and discussion of books that teach prayer, counseling, evangelism, and so on.

The charismatic movement was the first to employ these discipleship methods on a widespread scale. But in the 1980s other evangelical groups have adopted these same techniques in various ways, both formal and informal. Scores of "house churches" have sprung up from the discipleship groups.

Harry C. Griffith touches on a few of the objectives of a discipling group:

We are coming to understand that Christian discipleship implies....maturity. The disciples who lived with Jesus were led, over a period of three years, through an intensive training course which prepared them to live His message and to share it with the world. He led them toward *maturity*, toward the full development of their minds and spirits as they experienced life and coped with it through God's grace....

Discipleship also implies *discipline*, and discipline implies two more things. It indicates a willingness to follow a certain way, an obedience to the leader and conformity with his principles. It also suggests diligence to understand the ways of the leader and to incorporate them into one's own life.

Discipleship implies *sacrifice*. To follow another obediently and experience life reflectively, one must expect that sacrifice will be a part of the process....[1]

Obviously, this sort of intensive training experience calls for a leader with wisdom, compassion, and a clear calling to teach. The discipling experience tests the consecration of the leader as much as it tests the learners'. In fact, most discipling groups require the leader to carry out the same discipleship exercises and be subject to the same devotional disciplines that are expected of the rest of the group; and if the leader falls short at any point, the rest of the group will point out his or her laxity and call him or her to renewed obedience to the Lord. By no means is the leader an autocrat in the discipling group. The leader functions rather as a model, a moderator, and occasionally as a goad, but in no case should the group regard the discipling leader as a cult figure to be adored. Only the Lord Jesus is worthy of that.

With this pattern firmly in mind, we begin to understand the need for discipling books that are biblically based, practically oriented, and clearly written. Since the leader is not providing the contents from his or her own life, the group must look to the Bible for the contents of its study; and good discipleship resources should help them delve into the Bible to this end.

In this chapter we will consider some of the resources that are tailored to group discussion, with discipleship exercises to be implemented between meetings. LeRoy Eims simply defines *discipleship* as "living under the lordship of Christ."[2] The resources listed at the end of this chapter are designed to help us do exactly that: Learn to live in submission to the lordship of Christ, yet be accountable to another Christian (or group of Christians) who will be our spiritual yokefellows in the process of growing.

One of the foremost publishers of discipleship resources is NavPress, the publishing arm of the Navigators. Headquartered in Colorado Springs, this organization was started to lead servicemen to Christ during World War II. Since that time, it has branched into various kinds of personal evangelism and discipleship ministries. Navigator home Bible studies seem to reach professional people far more effectively than many church programs do.

---

[1] Harry C. Griffith, *Adventure in Discipleship* (Grand Rapids: Zondervan, 1978), pp. v–vi.
[2] LeRoy Eims, *What Every Christian Should Know about Growing* (Wheaton IL: Victor Books, 1982), p. 74 ff.

The Navigators draw upon nearly half a century of experience in personal evangelism and discipleship training to produce the discipleship books they have published. I recommend their training programs and their discipleship resources.

InterVarsity Christian Fellowship, a campus ministry begun in England and now active in the United States, is also a foremost publisher of discipleship resources. Most of IVCF's discipleship books have a clearly collegiate orientation; but I think they can still be used by laypersons outside the college setting.

A few denominational houses have also begun to produce discipleship resources that train young Christians in the foundational truths of the Christian faith and give them some orientation to the distinctive doctrines and traditions of their denominations. I have not attempted to list these denominational resources here, but you may check with your church publishing house for a list of resources that are designed for people from your denominational tradition.

I hope that by reviewing the bibliography of discipleship resources you will be reminded that the devotional life is best lived in fellowship with other Christians. A life committed to serving God and growing in the spiritual graces will require the guidance and encouragement of other Christians who are on the same journey, especially those who are a bit farther along on the journey. I hope this brief chapter sparks your interest in a discipleship group if you are not already involved in one. I believe this is an opportunity for Christian growth that every Christian should experience.

ANNOTATED BIBLIOGRAPHY

Eims, LeRoy. *The Lost Art of Disciple Making*. Grand Rapids: Zondervan, 1978.

An executive with the Navigators, Dr. Eims points to the need for effective follow-up with new converts, to be sure they get well rooted in Christ. He proposes a program of identifying and training new Christians through a one-to-one relationship with a more mature Christian. The goal of this program is to help the new convert reach a spiritual maturity that will allow her or him to disciple another new convert, so that the spiritual training effort will multiply. Eims believes this is Christ's intended pattern for Christian nurture, since it is the method Jesus himself used in training the Twelve.

Eims, LeRoy. *What Every Christian Should Know about Growing: Basic Steps to Discipleship*. Wheaton IL: Victor Books, 1976.

Designed to be a brief course in the rudiments of Christian growth, this book is divided into thirteen sections, appropriate for a quarterly adult study. Eims discusses how to study the Bible, how to pray, how to prevail over temptation, how to witness, and other foundational aspects of the Christian life.

Victor Books also publishes a leader's guide to be used with this book.

Griffith, Harry C. *Adventure in Discipleship*. Grand Rapids: Zondervan, 1978.

This forty-week study can be used by an individual or by a group. It assumes that the reader is a new convert who wants an introductory course in the teachings of Christ and training in the basic disciplines of Christian living. So the premise of this book is much the same as Eims's *What Every Christian Should Know about Growing*; but Griffith's study covers a much longer span of time (three quarters of a year) and deals with a broader range of concerns. Unfortunately, the publisher has not provided a leader's guide for Griffith's book; but a few questions at the end of each chapter may help launch group discussion.

Henrichsen, Walter A. *How to Disciple Your Children*. Wheaton IL: Victor Books, 1982.

Henrichsen, a long-time staff member with the Navigators, explains that the Christian family is the most natural setting for discipleship training. Children learn to imitate their parents; and if a Christian parent makes an intentional effort to convey a Christian lifestyle to the child, that child is likely to commit his or her life to Christ. Henrichsen deals with Christian parents' expectations (and occasional disappointments) in an enlightening way. This book could be a useful training manual for parents who want to begin a daily family devotional time; it gives a sound biblical and theological rationale for Christian child rearing.

Peterson, Eugene H. *A Long Obedience in the Same Direction*. Downers Grove IL: InterVarsity, 1980.

Peterson derives sixteen discipleship studies from the book of Psalms, which chronicles the strivings of several ancient writers who tried to grow in conformity to God's will. The author does not provide discussion questions, yet his book would be quite appropriate for group study.

Snyder, Pamela E. *A Life Styled by God*. Grand Rapids: Zondervan, 1985.

A part of Zondervan's popular "Woman's Workshop" series of discipleship books, this volume focuses on "spiritual discipline for weight control." Snyder explains how to displace unhealthy eating habits with healthy ones, how to deal with stress without turning to food, and how to form a women's group that will pursue spiritual growth and physical health, including weight loss. As with other books in this series, *A Life Styled by God* offers workbook activities to test your knowledge of what you read and to prompt further thinking. It is an effective group study resource.

Wilson, Earl D. *The Undivided Self.* Downers Grove IL: InterVarsity, 1983.

These fourteen studies deal with a problem common to Christians—the ambivalent desire to serve God yet serve oneself. The apostle Paul (Rom. 7:19) and countless other Christians have confessed that they have a divided mind. How can one resolve the tension? These studies provide some interesting insights that could be the springboard to lively group discussion.

Chapter Eleven
Family Worship Resources

Christian parents feel they ought to have a regular family devotional time, but few ever establish one. Why?

We might name several reasons: Busy schedule, fatigue at the end of the day, fidgety children, and uncertainty about what to do. These problems may have blocked your family from starting a regular devotional time. Or perhaps other difficulties have frustrated your efforts to lead the family in devotions. Let us consider the advantages of having a regular family devotional time, however; and then let us see what we can do to overcome the obstacles.

Any Christian parent can see the value in having a regular time for family Bible study, prayer, and discussion of spiritual matters. What better discipling group could there be than the family circle? Here children learn their life values, express their aspirations, and seek counsel for the problems they experience as they enter the world of human relationships. A wise Christian parent can use this quiet time of family togetherness to promote Christian values.

I know one couple who have raised more than a dozen foster children in their home, along with three children of their own. They have involved the foster children in their nightly devotions, teaching them God's Word and praying with them. Most of these children are now grown, scattered in schools and other homes where they may not see these foster parents again. Yet I am sure the influence of these Christian parents will have a continuing effect on those young people's lives. I can see the results of their godly teaching in the lives of their own three children, who have now reached their teen-age years and are setting a fine example as Christian young people. Surely the devotional time this family has each evening will touch the lives of several families. It is the best kind of evangelism, putting the good news in the very fiber of young lives.

I know another family that has a devotional time each day, led by the single parent who keeps a busy work schedule in addition to cleaning house, mending clothes, cooking meals, and carrying out the other chores associated with a full-time homemaker's routine. This young mother would have good reason to avoid adding any activities to her daily regimen. Yet she keeps a quarter-hour reserved for devotions with her children each evening, no matter how tired she may be. Her children are still quite small, perhaps several years away from making any decision for Christ; yet their mother's priorities must make a deep impression on their minds. They will grow up knowing that a daily quiet time with the Lord is vital, no matter how pressing the other demands of life may be.

Such examples convince me that a daily devotional time is within the reach of every family, as soon as we realize the benefits that can be obtained in this way. The foster couple and the single mother prove that we can overcome obstacles to family devotions when we make family worship a high priority, and we will make it a high priority when we understand the impact that family worship can have upon our lives.

Parents also grow in family devotions. Ethel L. Herr confesses:

> My husband and I entered parenthood with high ideals and a noble sense of mission. For our motto we took the Bible admonition to "train up a child in the way he should go: and when he is old, he will not depart from it" (Prov. 22:6, KJV). We expected through discipline, example, and consistent training to raise a family of dedicated Christians. These we defined as adults whose pathway of life paralleled our own, at least in religious matters.
>
> Convinced of the proverbial truth, "As the twig is bent, so grows the tree," we recognized our function to be the bending of twigs. We gave little consideration to our own need to bend and grow. Like older, stronger trees in a forest, we felt we stood tall enough to see what life was all about.
>
> Over the years our attitudes have changed. Our failures have humbled us. Successes have pointed us in new directions. Seeing ourselves as immature and needing growth has helped us to put the children in a better perspective. No longer do we look upon them as trainees but as persons....
>
> In dozens of compelling ways, our little teachers have taught us that the goal of parenthood is not to reproduce ourselves in carbon-copy models of Christian virtue. Rather, the goal of the family is maturity for each individual and for the family as a living, growing unit.[1]

When we look upon the family devotional time as not only a teaching time but a learning time, a time when all of us learn to grow in the graces of the Lord, we begin to relish family worship time and bring our most creative ideas to it. We begin to sense the Lord's presence in our midst when we meet in the family circle for worship, so we look forward to family devotions as a time we can share the delightful fellowship of Christ.

---

[1] Ethel L. Herr, *Growing Up Is a Family Affair* (Chicago: Moody, 1978), pp. 9–10.

Recognizing Children's Needs and Abilities

A wise parent begins to discern that the family devotional time must be structured in a way that meets a child's needs and abilities at each stage of life. A preschooler for example cannot read and memorize Scripture verses, but he or she can draw pictures to illustrate the Bible stories you read to him or her. A teen-ager may be bored by doing artwork or crafts at family devotions; but she or he may be deeply engrossed by a serious discussion of marriage, choosing a career, or some other issue that confronts her or him now. Be alert to the needs of each member of the family, and try to scale your worship activities to suit those needs.

Fortunately, Christian publishers have recognized the need to provide family devotional resources that are tailor-made for children of each age level. Standard Press has prepared a series of family devotional books with this in mind, and other publishers are following suit. The years ahead should see a wealth of family devotional resources coming from the leading publishers, and this will help you in designing your family worship activities. Maxine Hancock gives an example of how she has provided a variety of worship activities for her preschool children:

> Beyond the daily routine of Scripture reading, Christian parents will find many opportunities to widen their children's experience with the Bible and its truths. Reading from storybooks and listening to records or tapes with the children are some possibilities. One of our preschoolers has listened, engrossed, to whole books of the Bible on the *Living Bible* cassettes. Roleplaying and informal dramatizations of many of the stories has been fun. For a few favorite stories I give the children flannelgraph figures to work with.[2]

Be creative. Reading the Bible or a Bible storybook is a very easy way to conduct family devotions, a way that children will often enjoy. But be ready to try some other activities as a family that will allow you to express your praise for the Lord and to learn more about him.

Choosing a Bible Version

One of the most important decisions you will make as you begin to establish a family devotional time is, Which Bible version shall be read? In my earlier book, *Bible Study Resource Guide* (Nashville: Thomas Nelson, 1982), I dealt with the matter of choosing a Bible version for serious study or for devotional reading. But when you choose a Bible version to read during your family devotions, I suggest you bring some additional concerns to the decision:

Is it easy to memorize? The standard Bible versions such as the KJV, RSV, and

---

[2]Maxine Hancock, *People in Process* (Old Tappan NJ: Fleming H. Revell, 1978), p. 93.

NASV are careful to follow the meaning of the original Hebrew and Greek texts; but they can be rather awkward for a child to memorize. More modern versions such as the NIV, NKJV, and TEV are written in everyday language that children can readily understand and memorize. I suggest that you try one of these versions if you plan to make Bible memorization a part of your family devotional time.

Does it have subheadings and paragraphs? These topic divisions decide what sections of Scripture to read for your family devotional time. If you are not familiar with the Bible, these divisions can help you decide where to focus the family's attention as you study a given subject.

Aside from the question of which version you should use, consider these matters of format and quality:

Is the print large enough to be read easily? Advertisers tell us that large-print editions of the Bible are ideal for older folks who have poor eyesight, but they are also ideal for young children just learning to read. If you plan to have your children read from the Bible at some point, be sure the Bible has large type that will not strain their eyes.

Is it durable? You may have an exquisite family Bible with fine leather binding, gilt edges, and other expensive features. Such a Bible makes a beautiful conversation piece for the coffee table, but I would not recommend it for your family devotional reading. It's better to have an inexpensive Bible with a durable cover (flexible Kivar or Kivartext on boards), which will stand up to rugged handling as it is passed from one family member to another—and occasionally dropped. If you are worried that someone will damage the Bible while it is being passed around, your family members will sense your apprehension; so why not get an inexpensive, yet sturdy book that will stand up to regular use?

The brief comments I have made here are intended to help you deal with some of the first questions that come to a parent's mind when thinking about a family devotional time. By no means is this a complete guide to conducting family worship. But among the books listed in the bibliography, you will find more thorough and helpful books to help you get started.

ANNOTATED BIBLIOGRAPHY

Brandt, Catharine. *We Light the Candles*. Minneapolis: Augsburg, 1976.

Brandt has given us a useful activity book that families can use for devotions in the weeks of Advent. The activities focus on the Advent wreath and the meaning of each candle lit in celebration of our Lord's birth. Even the youngest children can learn from these devotionals.

Brock, Raymond T. *The Christ Centered Family*. Springfield MO: Gospel Publishing House, 1977.

This small volume serves as a fitting primer for Christian parents who want to raise their children with reverence for God. Brock discusses the dynamics of a Christian marriage before and after children enter the picture. He considers the different kinds of spiritual leadership that the mother and father should provide for their children. And he suggests activities that a family can use to focus their lives around the lordship of Christ. Brock respects conservative evangelical ideals for family living.

Conway, Jim, et. al. *Your Family: A Love and Maintenance Manual for People with Parents and Other Relatives*. Downers Grove IL: InterVarsity, 1982.

Most books about the Christian family are addressed to the parents, but here is one directed to the children—specifically, college-age children. This compilation of articles from *HIS Magazine* (published by InterVarsity Christian Fellowship) deals with the tensions that most Christian young people experience as they enter their late teens and take their first tentative steps away from home. Written for the evangelical teen-ager, *Your Family* could make an excellent gift.

Cook, Walter L. *Table Prayers for the Family Circle*. Grand Rapids: Baker, 1982.

Cook provides 160 prayers appropriate for mealtime worship or for the family altar. Each selection consists of only three sentences, offering thanks for some aspect of God's blessing.

Klug, Ron and Lyn Klug, eds. *The Christian Family Bedtime Reading Book*. Minneapolis: Augsburg, 1982.

A collection of stories, prayers, poems, and songs that parents and small children can share at bedtime. Each evening's material focuses on an important facet of Christian living. This is a good starter book for families that want to establish a nightly time of devotions.

Lewis, Margie M. *The Hurting Parent*. Grand Rapids: Zondervan, 1980.

Lewis focuses on the emotional stresses that are a normal (yet heartbreaking) aspect of raising a family. She deals especially with the problems parents may encounter with teen-agers. A sensitive and helpful book.

Martin, Paul. *Devotions for Today's Family*. Grand Rapids: Baker, 1977.

A set of simple, informal readings for the family's mealtime devotions. Martin provides material that children can understand yet youth and adults can take to heart as well.

Rickerson, Wayne. *Christian Family Activities for Families with Preschoolers*.

Cincinnati: Standard Publishing, 1982.

This workbook contains everything that parents of preschoolers would need to conduct a nightly devotional time with their children—including craft materials to cut out and assemble. A full year's activities are included. This is an excellent family devotional resource.[3]

Rinker, Rosalind. *How to Have Family Prayers*. Grand Rapids: Zondervan, 1977.

Rinker provides very simple instructions for starting a family devotional time, including a program of activities for the first month of family worship. Families that are eager to know how to begin a daily devotional time will find much practical help in this book.

Shibley, David and Naomi Shibley. *More Special Times with God*. Nashville: Thomas Nelson, 1984.

This sequel to the Shibley's popular book *Special Times with God* is also designed for parents to use in family devotions with young children. Each reading in this book is a story about an important Bible character. Sure to arrest the attention of even the liveliest child, these stories teach valuable truths about the way God's people are called to live.

Shibley, David and Naomi Shibley. *Special Times with God*. Nashville: Thomas Nelson, 1983.

Here is a book that parents of young children can read aloud for family devotions each evening. Each reading lifts up an important lesson in Christian living that children can apply to their own lives, even in preschool years.

Souter, John C. and James O'Brosky. *A Family Hour Notebook: Getting to Know God*. Irvine CA: Harvest House, 1978.

A workbook designed for family Bible study, this provides cut-outs and game materials that bring variety to the activities. Souter and O'Brosky encourage churches to use this workbook for once-a-week family worship times. Eighteen sessions are included. The series explores the nature of God and his relationship with us.

Swindoll, Charles R. *Home—Where Life Makes Up Its Mind*. Portland: Multnomah, 1979.

Swindoll shares his deepest convictions about the importance of a conse-

---

[3]This is the first in a series of four activity books that Standard publishes for various family situations. The other volumes are: *Christian Family Activities for Families with Children* (1982) and *Christian Family Activities for Families with Teens* (1982), both by Wayne Rickerson, and Bobbie Reed's *Christian Family Activities for One-Parent Families* (1982).

crated Christian home. Directing his words to parents, he stresses the vital need for training children to respect Christian values and to understand the gospel of Jesus Christ. Richly illustrated.

Ward, Ruth. *Devotions: A Family Affair*. Grand Rapids: Baker, 1981.

Ward gives sound advice about starting a family devotional time. She deals with many of the issues raised in Chapter 1 of this *Resource Guide*, but in the specific context of family devotional worship. It is well to read this book before attempting a family devotional time; it could help you avoid obstacles that can dampen the project at the outset.

White, Mary. *Successful Family Devotions*. Colorado Springs: NavPress, 1981.

White discusses some of the special challenges that parents will face as they try to lead family devotions at each stage of their children's lives, from preschool years to college age. She gives some good advice for coping with the boredom, bewilderment, and occasional belligerence that children might show toward the discipline of family devotions. She paints a hopeful picture of the benefits that a family can derive from a daily devotional time; but she is realistic enough to concede that conflicts will arise. "Success" in this endeavor has to be measured in the long-term spiritual growth of the family, rather than in the level of gratification each session may bring.

Author Index

Title Index

Notes

Notes

Notes

Notes

Notes

Notes

Notes

Notes

Notes

Notes